microwave
MUG SOUPS

microwave
MUG SOUPS

home-made in minutes ....
with just a mug to wash up!

50 delicious recipes from
round the world

THEO MICHAELS

LORENZ BOOKS

CONTENTS

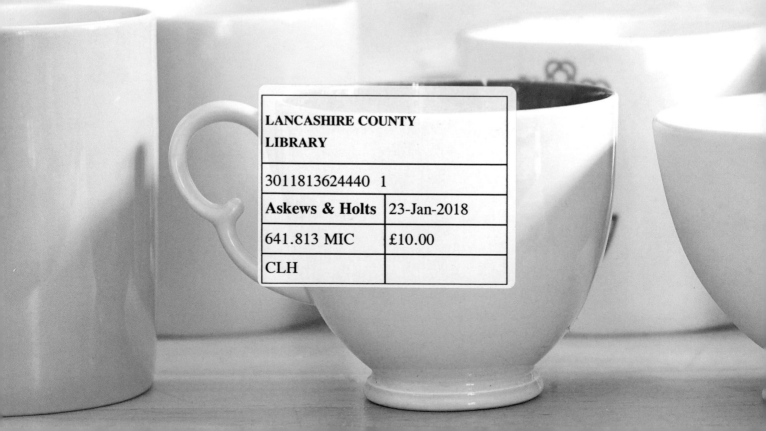

INTRODUCTION

This cookbook is all about innovative recipes that meet the reality of modern life. Fast, healthy (there are a couple of exceptions!) soups cooked in a matter of minutes, using almost all fresh ingredients. The microwave has come a long way since its early incarnations a couple of decades ago, and there are health as well as speed benefits to be had, with more nutrients retained, especially when it comes to cooking vegetables.

Soup is the ultimate comfort food. Whether you yearn for a traditional cream of tomato, a spicy fish chowder or a deliciously umami-rich ramen – a mug of soup is the perfect supper on the sofa. But making a great soup can be an arduous task: an elongated process of slow cooking, blending and finally ending up with more soup than you can give away. Well let's put an end to all that malarkey! Now you can make your favourite mug soup in just a matter of minutes and without tons of washing up. Using fresh, natural ingredients with a few cheats along the way you can enjoy a delicious soup knowing exactly what's in it – the perfect quick fix!

The soup recipes in this book have been specially created to suit the microwave and to be cooked in a single mug, ready to eat. They are all speedy and simple, but most importantly, taste fantastic. Instead of opening up a can, you can have an even yummier home-cooked borscht, or chicken, even minestrone – made fresh in just the same amount of time.

I've created a great range of choices for you, from simple creamy soups like asparagus and cream cheese, potato and leek, and mushroom, to super-spicy Caribbean chilli chicken, hot and sour broth, Szechuan hot pot... There are classic soups from round the world to try, Moroccan chickpea, caldo verde from Portugal, Cambodian seafood, green Thai curry, kjotsupa from Iceland, kapusniak from Poland... You'll find both tempting indulgent soups, and good-for-you soups packed with lots of green things!

There have been challenges in making soups from scratch in the microwave. One obstacle was avoiding the use of a blender. The last thing I wanted was everyone to cook a microwave mug soup and then starting mucking about trying to blend it! So I've boycotted the blender for my microwave mug soups. There was also lots of research along the way to acheive the same depth of flavour you normally get from slow cooking. This is where a really good stock is invaluable, plus a few tricks that really help pack your mug soup with punch.

As always, I hope this book will be your loyal kitchen companion – a good cookbook in my house is covered in splashes, stains and comments; a sign that it is being used and enjoyed.

FINALLY:

No recipe is foolproof; whether you are cooking in a conventional oven, under a grill, or boiling water on the hob. Cooking means using ingredients. And ingredients are a natural product; they vary in quality, texture, size, density, starting temperature... your ingredients might weigh exactly 50 grams but might be cut slightly thinner or thicker than mine and take a fraction less or more to cook.

Cooking is also a very personal thing. How many times have you eaten the same thing as someone else and while you loved or hated it, the other person felt the exact opposite! This is especially obvious when it comes to things like adding chilli to a dish; some like it hot, some not so much... As with all cookbooks, taste the recipe, tweak it to your preferences and feel free to treat all the recipes as a guide. If I've specified asparagus and you really prefer broad beans – go ahead!

This is a quick guide to the basics of microwave mug cooking. Using a microwave is a bit more precise than cooking on the hob or in the oven, so do refer to the manufacturer's instructions for your own machine. There are hints and tips here to help you along the way.

HOW TO USE THIS BOOK

CHOOSING MUGS:

I've tried to keep every recipe in my book easy and to use standard mugs that most people have in their cupboard. All the recipes are cooked in a standard 300ml/½ pint mug. Each recipe specifies the minimum size though you can use a larger mug if preferred, or of course you can cook in any type of microwave-safe bowl or container. Bigger is usually better.

If possible always try to choose a wider mug rather than a tall and thin one, as a wider mug invariably cooks the meal more evenly and reduces the chances of overspills, whereas tall mugs tend to boil over much more easily. Always be sure to put your mug on a microwaveable plate to catch any overspills.

Not everything is suitable to cook in the microwave – any metal container for instance is a big no-no! Make sure it has no metallic or gilt decorations. If you are unsure whether a mug is microwave safe just check underneath; most will say on the base whether they can be used in the microwave. And of course cutlery should never be microwaved.

A NOTE ON INGREDIENT MEASUREMENTS:

The recipes give imperial, metric and American cup measurements for some ingredients – these are specific sizes (not the same as the mug you are making your soup in!). An American culinary cup is 240ml.

MICROWAVE KNOW-HOW:

Microwaves are now super-sophisticated; many have oven settings, grills, and various power settings. Most people I know still end up just using a fraction of the options available. As such, I've avoided any fancy business in my book – all recipes are based on 800w. If you have a microwave with less power then you will need to increase the cooking time, but do it in intervals: an extra 30 seconds here or there, and take out the meal to check whether it needs longer.

Two identical microwaves can still vary slightly; your microwave may be 800w like mine but might in reality be slightly hotter or cooler. You might find that your microwave has certain hot-spots.

Equally if you have a rocket-fuelled super powerful microwave you'll need to reduce the cooking time and again, I would do this in intervals; if my recipe calls for 2 minutes and your microwave is much more powerful, try a minute first and see if it needs longer. Cooking in the microwave is a bit like seasoning – you can always cook more but you can't cook less. To avoid overcooking I would always err on the side of caution, increasing the cooking time minimally and then testing it. If it isn't cooked you can cook it a bit more. If it is over-cooked, you're starting again…

All the recipes in this book are cooked uncovered unless specified. The mug or dish is always covered with clear film or plastic wrap and pierced with a knife to give a small vent.

SAFETY FIRST:

The nature of microwave cooking means ingredients, food and the vessels can get extremely hot. Always handle with care and use oven gloves or a dish towel to remove vessels from the microwave.

Keep your face away from just-microwaved food, especially for dishes that have been cooked for several minutes or more and require immediate stirring – they can splash or spit.

When eating microwave food, sometimes there are pockets of heat within the dish that are hotter than the rest, so stir first and please eat slowly. Where the recipe states the dish must stand after cooking, let it stand – it will be hot, hot, hot.

ADAPTING QUANTITIES:

All my recipes are for one person, however, there is nothing stopping you from making two or three mug soups at the same time and putting them in the microwave all at once to cook. If you add more than one mug the microwave needs to work harder to cook larger quantities which means you will need to increase your cooking times slightly.

Do note it isn't a simple case of doubling the quantity and then doubling the cooking time – it doesn't work like that. So, if you are cooking more than one mug at a time, increase the time by about 25–30% and see if it needs longer. If it normally takes 3 minutes in the microwave for one mug, and I was cooking two mugs at the same time, I would microwave it for about 3 minutes 45 seconds and see how it looks, then cook longer if needed. If my recipe calls for 2 minutes in the microwave and you are cooking three mugs at once, you will probably need to increase this to 3 or 4 minutes.

TO BLEND OR NOT TO BLEND:

Traditionally cooked soups (i.e cooked in a pan on the hob) usually end up being blended. I have purposely avoided doing this for the purposes of integrity – what's the point of cooking a 3-minute soup in the mug from scratch to then start getting out the blender! You can do this if you wish of course, but instead I've used a couple of different techniques:

1. **Long-cook** – some ingredients when cooked long enough (like potatoes) break down and can be mashed with the back of a fork to get a smooth consistency.
2. **Breadcrumbs** – using these as a thickening agent works very well for microwave mug soups, and incidentally is also a very traditional means of thickening some soups and sauces.
3. **Going chunky** – there's nothing wrong with having something to chew on!
4. **Flour** – I've used a combination of cornflour/cornstarch and flour in some of my microwave mug soup recipes as a means to help thicken the soup or give it a little more body. Adding cornflour tends to thicken the soup with a slightly more gelatinous feel, and once cooked won't cloud the soup. Whereas using plain/all-purpose flour will also thicken the soup but does tend to remain cloudy (which is fine if the soup isn't clear anyway).

A good stock is the backbone of any decent soup. If you have some leftover chicken bones and scraps of meat from a roast chicken then taking a few minutes to make your own stock is great. It's natural, home-made and you know exactly what's in it. The other good thing is once you've made the chicken stock you can let it cool, pop it into a container and freeze it for another day.

THE SOUP-ER STOCK

To get the most out of a microwave mug soup I personally always use chicken stock (unless expressly stated to use water or a different stock), even for the seafood and vegetarian soups although of course you wouldn't use it in the latter if cooking vegetarian. Where the book states a stock, it is easiest to use a stock or bouillon cube added to hot water, or break off a pinch of stock cube and add it to your mug – unless you have some home-made stock to hand, which is best of all. And as you'd expect, that is something you can also make quickly and easily in the microwave.

Making your own chicken 'bone broth' (that's stock to you and me) is as therapeutic as it is satisfying. Here's a quick microwave version to get you started. I've kept this recipe as simple as possible, but you can add other ingredients as you would when making a stock in the traditional way. If you want to keep it super-simple then just follow this recipe; if you have time, microwave some diced root vegetables (carrot, onion, celery, etc) first for a couple of minutes and add to the bone mixture.

You do really need to use leftover chicken bones from a roast (if you have too many you can freeze the chicken bones to use another day). One special tip is to add any leftover chicken skin from your roast dinner as that will really boost the flavour.

65g/2½oz cooked chicken bones
250ml/8fl oz/1 cup water
Pinch of salt and pepper
½ clove garlic

Just combine all the ingredients in a mug or container and microwave uncovered for 5 minutes (put the mug on a plate to catch any overspill). Strain and use as required. That's it!

THE CLASSICS

When it comes to soup everyone has their favourite, but there are some soups that have become firmly established go-to bowls (or mugs!) of comfort. Tomato, creamy chicken, mushroom, ramen... I've adapted these best-loved recipes so you can now make your own versions in a matter of minutes – and all with fresh ingredients!

This just tastes so good! The chief tasting officer (my daughter Eva) devoured this one which was a good sign as Cream of Tomato is her favourite soup... ever!

CREAM OF TOMATO SOUP

SERVES: 1
COOKING TIME: 2½–3 minutes
EQUIPMENT: 300ml/½ pint mug

½ clove garlic, diced
7.5ml/1½ tsp tomato purée
7.5ml/1½ tsp olive oil
2.5ml/½ tsp ground cumin
2.5ml/½ tsp cumin seeds, whole

185ml/6fl oz/¾ cup passata/ bottled strained tomatoes
2.5ml/½ tsp sugar
45ml/3 tbsp double/heavy cream
100ml/3½fl oz/scant ½ cup stock
Seasoning

1 Add the garlic, tomato purée, olive oil, ground cumin and seeds to a mug and microwave, uncovered for 1 minute.

2 Add the passata, seasoning and sugar and microwave for 90 seconds uncovered.

3 Finish the soup by pouring over the cream and enough stock to fill your mug. If not warm enough microwave again for 30 seconds. Season again and serve with crusty bread.

CHEF'S NOTES:
There is nothing I can add – cream of tomato soup – a classic! Although now I think about it... get the best quality passata you can afford; it'll make all the difference.

Cream of chicken soup needs no introduction. Creamy, warming, the only accompaniment needed is a blanket and a good film… (oh, and maybe some nice bread to dip!).

CREAM OF CHICKEN SOUP

1 Add the olive oil, celery, leek, carrot and seasoning to a mug and microwave, covered for 90 seconds.

2 Add the chicken and flour and mix thoroughly, followed by 90ml/3fl oz/generous ⅓ cup stock. Microwave, uncovered, for 2 minutes.

3 Add the remaining stock (or enough to fill the mug) and the cream, and microwave for a further 30 seconds to warm through, if needed.

4 Garnish with more black pepper, salt and fresh thyme sprigs.

CHEF'S NOTES:
To reduce the richness, swap the cream for milk.

SERVES: 1
COOKING TIME: 3½–4 minutes
EQUIPMENT: 300ml/½ pint mug

7.5ml/1½ tsp olive oil
6g/¼oz celery, diced
6g/¼oz leek, diced
6g/¼oz carrot, diced

35g/1½oz chicken breast, diced
7.5ml/1½ tsp plain/all-purpose flour
215ml/7½fl oz/scant 1 cup stock
7.5ml/1½ tsp cream
Fresh thyme sprigs, to garnish
Seasoning

Minestrone soup was born out of the necessity to use up leftovers.
Originating in Italy, pasta, beans and chunky vegetables were commonly
found in the 'leftovers soup'. Since then minestrone soup has become a
classic and enjoyed the world over.

MINESTRONE SOUP

1 Add the olive oil, celery, leek, carrot, onion, garlic,
pancetta and seasoning to a mug and microwave,
covered, for 2 minutes.

2 Add the tomatoes, tomato purée, peas, spaghetti
and a third of the stock (60ml/2fl oz), cover and
microwave for 4 minutes.

3 Top up with another third of the stock and
microwave, covered, for another 2 minutes, before
resting for a minute.

4 Finally add the parsley and top with the remaining
stock, season to taste and garnish with the grated
Parmesan cheese.

CHEF'S NOTES:
This is perfect to use up leftover cooked spaghetti – if
so, you can reduce the second microwave cooking
period to just 1 minute.

Add a pinch of dried chilli flakes for a little oomph
and a drizzle of olive oil over the top.

SERVES: 1
**COOKING TIME: 8 minutes,
    plus 1 minute resting**
**EQUIPMENT: 300ml/½ pint
    mug**

7.5ml/1½ tsp olive oil
10g/⅓oz celery, diced
10g/⅓oz leek, diced
10g/⅓oz carrot, diced
10g/⅓oz onion, diced
½ clove garlic, sliced
20g/¾oz smoked pancetta
    (or bacon), diced

2 cherry tomatoes (about
    25g/½oz), diced
5ml/½ tsp tomato purée
50g/1oz frozen peas
8g/⅓oz broken quick-cook
    spaghetti
180ml/6fl oz/¾ cup stock
15ml/1 tbsp chopped fresh
    parsley
15ml/1 tbsp Parmesan
    cheese, grated
Seasoning

When I asked my wife what her favourite soup was, her reply was quick and succinct: "Potato and leek – and don't muck about with it!" A classic marriage of flavours that needs no introduction – but I've written one anyway.

POTATO AND LEEK SOUP

1 Add the garlic, leek, butter and a pinch of seasoning to a mug and microwave, covered, for 2 minutes.

2 Then add the potato, flour, milk and a third (about 50–60ml) of the stock, and microwave covered, for 5 minutes.

3 Once cooked mix thoroughly and break up the potato with the back of a fork to help thicken the soup.

4 Finally add the remaining stock, mix thoroughly and microwave again for 30 seconds just to warm through (if using hot stock you needn't microwave again at this stage). Serve with bread rolls, if you like.

CHEF'S NOTES:
For an extra-rich soup add a little knob of butter at the end of cooking.

SERVES: 1
COOKING TIME: 7–7½ minutes
EQUIPMENT: 300ml/½ pint
   mug

¼ clove garlic, diced
30g/1oz leek, diced
15ml/1 tbsp butter
100g/3¾oz potato,
   diced roughly into 1cm/
   ½in cubes
15ml/1 tbsp plain/all-purpose
   flour
30ml/2 tbsp milk
150ml/5fl oz/⅔ cup stock
Seasoning

I love French onion soup but was dubious I could get the depth of taste in a couple of minutes in the microwave when it usually takes so much longer to achieve on the stove. But this recipe is full of flavour! And it goes without saying that no self-respecting French onion soup would be complete without croûtons.

FRENCH ONION SOUP – WITH CROÛTONS

1 Add the onion, seasoning, olive oil and butter to a mug and microwave, covered, for 4 minutes. If your onions are not golden, microwave again for a further minute, but be careful not to burn.

2 Now add the flour, stock and brandy to the onions and microwave again, uncovered, for 30 seconds to warm through. Leave to rest while you make the croûtons.

3 To make the croûtons, place the bread squares in the microwave (on a plate or straight in there) for 30 seconds. The croûtons won't toast but will cook and start to become brittle. You can also sprinkle grated cheese over the bread squares before microwaving, to make cheesy croûtons.

4 Then place the croûtons gently on top of the cooked soup and garnish with **extra cheese**.

CHEF'S NOTES:
If you don't have brandy try adding an equal quantity of white wine.

You can garnish with a scattering of finely chopped fresh parsley if available.

SERVES: 1
COOKING TIME: 5–6 minutes
EQUIPMENT: 300ml/½ pint mug

65g/2½oz white onion, thinly sliced
7.5ml/1½ tsp olive oil
7.5ml/1½ tsp butter
7.5ml/1½ tsp plain/all-purpose flour
125ml/4½fl oz/½ cup beef stock
2.5ml/½ tsp brandy
½ slice bread, cut into 2.5cm/1in squares
Gruyère cheese, grated
Seasoning

Marrowfat peas once cooked turn into a silky sweet purée that makes the perfect base for this smoky pea and pancetta soup. A slightly different take on an old-time pea and ham classic.

SMOKY PEA AND PANCETTA SOUP

SERVES: 1
COOKING TIME: 4–4½ minutes
EQUIPMENT: 300ml/½ pint mug

½ clove garlic, diced
½ spring onion/scallion, sliced
5ml/1 tsp olive oil

15g/½oz pancetta (or smoked bacon), diced
180g/6¼oz marrowfat peas (canned)
120ml/4fl oz/½ cup stock
2.5ml/½ tsp smoked paprika, plus extra to garnish
2.5ml/½ tsp butter
Seasoning

CHEF'S NOTES:
You can always omit the pancetta or bacon for a simple vegetarian pea soup – if so, I would increase the smoked paprika by a pinch to keep the smoky flavour.

For even more convenience, you can always add pre-cooked smoked ham at the very end instead of the pancetta.

1 Add the garlic, spring onion, olive oil and pancetta or bacon, and microwave uncovered for 1 minute.

2 Add the peas, half the stock and the paprika and microwave covered for 3 minutes.

3 Mash the peas with the back of a fork as much as possible, season generously, add the butter and the remaining stock and microwave for 30 seconds, if needed to warm through (you may not need to as the peas will be hot!).

4 Garnish with an extra pinch of paprika.

A perfect combination of tender broccoli and melted blue cheese create an unctuous soup to dip into – and a great way of using up blue cheese!

BROCCOLI AND BLUE CHEESE SOUP

1 Add the broccoli, garlic, onion, olive oil and 45ml/ 3 tbsp of stock to the mug, cover and microwave for 5 minutes (don't worry if it browns a little around the edges).

2 Now combine the milk with the cornflour and add to the mug. Stir thoroughly and microwave uncovered for 1 minute.

3 Add the blue cheese and microwave again, uncovered, for 30 seconds.

4 Season to taste and crumble a little cheese on top as a garnish.

CHEF'S NOTES:
Depending on how strong your blue cheese is, change the quantity to your preference.

SERVES: **1**
COOKING TIME: **6½ minutes**
EQUIPMENT: **300ml/½ pint mug**

50g/2oz broccoli, very finely chopped
½ clove garlic, diced
7.5ml/1½ tsp onion, diced
7.5ml/1½ tsp olive oil
195ml/7fl oz/scant 1 cup stock
15ml/1 tbsp milk
15ml/1 tbsp cornflour/ cornstarch
10g/⅓oz blue cheese, preferably Stilton
Seasoning

VEGETARIAN SOUPS

Vegetables, surprisingly, is the one food group that takes the longest to cook in the microwave. Soft vegetables such as asparagus and tomatoes are cooked incredibly fast, while root vegetables (carrots, potatoes, sweet potatoes and so on) are very dense and so the microwave has to work harder in shaking all those molecules to cook them; but the good thing is they still get cooked in a fraction of the time they usually take!

This warming soup of black pepper and spice is as good for the soul as it is for your body. Commonly known as Indian Pepper Water, there are dozens of variations of Milagu Rasam. But don't be put off by the list of ingredients – there are a few cheats in the Chef's Notes below.

MILAGU RASAM – INDIAN PEPPER WATER

SERVES: 1
COOKING TIME: 3–3½ minutes
EQUIPMENT: 300ml/½ pint mug

30g/1¼oz fresh tomatoes, chopped
15ml/1 tbsp chopped fresh coriander/cilantro stalks
185ml/6fl oz/¾ cup stock
7.5ml/1½ tsp tamarind paste

For the spice paste
½ clove garlic, diced
2.5ml/½ tsp mustard seeds
1.5ml/¼ tsp ground cumin
1.5ml/¼ tsp fennel seeds
1.5ml/¼ tsp ground black pepper
Generous pinch of chilli flakes
Generous pinch of turmeric
Generous pinch of asafoetida
Pinch of salt
5ml/1 tsp olive oil
2.5ml/½ tsp butter

1 Add all the spice paste ingredients to a mug, stir well and microwave uncovered for 90 seconds.

2 Then add the tomatoes and coriander stalks and microwave again for 1 minute uncovered.

3 Finally add the stock and tamarind paste and microwave for a further 30 seconds to 1 minute to warm through.

CHEF'S NOTES:
Try adding a few tablespoons of coconut milk for a creamier creation.

You can add desiccated/dry unsweetened shredded coconut for a thicker soup.

Tamarind paste – you can buy ready-made tamarind paste, alternatively you can purchase the dried tamarinds and soak in a little water to form a paste. If you don't have all those spices to hand, you could substitute them for some ready-made curry powder (using a teaspoon at first and adding more to taste) and replace the tamarind with a good squeeze of lime juice. Quite often when I cook with fresh coriander I'll use the stalks separately from the leaves. The leaves are a more delicate garnish whereas the stalks, which are packed with flavour, are a touch hardier so can take a little cooking.

I love this soup (as did my son Lex – but I think that's because he knew there was ale in it!). This soup has a totally unique texture and flavour unlike any other recipe in my book. The ale at the end slightly carbonates the soup making it extremely light and airy. Don't be tempted to put too much ale in as the soup will start to go bitter, but with just enough it's perfect.

CHEDDAR AND ALE SOUP

1 Add the butter to the mug and microwave uncovered for 30 seconds or until melted.

2 Add the flour to the butter and mix together to form a paste. Microwave again for 1 minute uncovered.

3 Slowly add the milk, a tablespoon at a time, stirring continuously. Once the milk is fully incorporated, microwave uncovered for 1 minute, remove, stir and microwave again for 30 seconds.

4 Now add the grated cheese and seasoning and combine thoroughly.

5 Finally pour in the ale and stir; the soup is ready.

6 Garnish with a pinch of seasoning (it can take a good amount of black pepper) and some celery fronds or even a pinch of celery salt, if liked.

CHEF'S NOTES:
Once you've opened a bottle of ale to use some in the soup I find the rest goes very well in a glass…

SERVES: **1**
COOKING TIME: **3 minutes**
EQUIPMENT: **300ml/½ pint mug**

15ml/1 tbsp butter
15ml/1 tbsp flour
125ml/4½fl oz/½ cup milk
25g/1oz Cheddar cheese, grated
30ml/2 tbsp ale (I use a golden ale)
Celery fronds, to garnish
Pinch of celery salt (optional)
Seasoning

This isn't a smooth pea purée; this is a chunky pea soup that tastes fresh and vibrant, with something to chew on! A marriage of flavours that work so well together – sometimes I can't resist adding a few chilli flakes at the end for a little kick.

CRUSHED PEA SOUP WITH FETA

SERVES: 1
COOKING TIME: 7½ minutes
EQUIPMENT: 300ml/½ pint
    mug

½ clove garlic, diced
½ spring onion/scallion,
    sliced
7.5ml/1½ tsp olive oil

75g/2½oz frozen peas
185ml/6fl oz/¾ cup stock
7.5ml/1½ tsp cornflour/
    cornstarch
3 chopped fresh mint leaves
15g/½oz feta cheese,
    crumbled
Seasoning

1 Add the garlic, spring onion, olive oil and seasoning to your mug and microwave uncovered for 1 minute.

2 Add the frozen peas and 60ml/4 tbsp of the stock and microwave, covered, for 5 minutes.

3 Mash the peas as much as you can with the back of a fork, it won't mash too much but that's OK as this is meant to be a chunky soup. Add the cornflour and the remaining stock and microwave uncovered for 90 seconds.

4 Finally stir through the chopped mint and feta, saving a little of both to garnish.

CHEF'S NOTES:
Try adding a few chilli flakes for some extra zing!

There are times when I crave something packed with goodness and want a real input of foliage – my soup-er green egg soup satisfies that craving whole-heartedly. There may seem like a ton of vegetation going into this soup but it cooks down a lot. Best eaten with a spoon and plenty of napkins.

SOUP-ER GREEN EGG SOUP

SERVES: 1
COOKING TIME: 3 minutes 45
    seconds, plus 3 minutes
    standing
EQUIPMENT: 300ml/½ pint
    mug

60g/2oz mixed baby leaves,
    such as kale, spinach, pea
    shoots, etc
A couple of sprigs fresh
    coriander/cilantro
A couple of sprigs fresh
    parsley
A couple of sprigs fresh dill
1 clove garlic, finely chopped
Pinch of chilli flakes
15ml/1 tbsp olive oil
150ml/5fl oz/⅔ cup stock
1 small egg
Seasoning

1 Finely chop the baby leaves and herbs, as much as you can (the finer the better), and add to your mug along with the garlic, chilli flakes, olive oil, seasoning and just over half the stock (about 90ml/6 tbsp), and microwave covered for 3 minutes.

2 Give the cooked greens a really good mash with the back of a fork before adding the remaining stock and stirring.

3 Gently crack the egg on to the mixture so it rests on the top (don't stir!), cover and microwave for 45 seconds or until the egg is just cooked (it will continue to cook as it rests in the hot soup).

4 Leave to stand for 3 minutes (it will be very hot!) and garnish with just a pinch more salt or chilli flakes.

CHEF'S NOTES:
You can really freestyle with this recipe in terms of what baby leaves and herbs you use. In saying that the dill is what brings the dish together so do include this if you can.
    A few drops of hot sauce goes great at the end!

I'm a huge fan of chipotle; the perfect combination of sweet, heat and smoke. My Mexican corn and chipotle soup makes for a hearty vegetarian dish packed with flavour and thick enough to chew...

MEXICAN CORN AND CHIPOTLE SOUP

1 Add all the ingredients to a mug except the fresh breadcrumbs and coriander, and only add 30ml/2 tbsp of the stock at this stage. Microwave covered for 5 minutes.

2 Add the remaining stock and stir through the breadcrumbs to thicken the soup. Check the temperature of the soup and microwave for 30 seconds if not hot enough.

3 Garnish with fresh coriander sprigs.

CHEF'S NOTES:
Use frozen corn kernels if more convenient. Chipotle paste is easily purchased from most supermarkets, but the heat does vary! Add more or less to your personal preference.

SERVES: **1**
COOKING TIME: **5–5½ minutes**
EQUIPMENT: **300ml/½ pint mug**

10g/⅓oz green bell pepper, diced
10g/⅓oz celery, finely diced
10g/⅓oz red onion, finely diced
1 clove garlic, finely chopped
7.5ml/1½ tsp olive oil
60g/2¼oz fresh corn kernels
Pinch of dried oregano
60ml/4 tbsp chopped canned tomatoes
150ml/5fl oz/⅔ cup stock
5ml/1 tsp chipotle paste
30ml/2 tbsp fresh breadcrumbs
Fresh coriander/cilantro sprigs, to garnish
Seasoning

A hearty yet still refined mushroom soup. It does take a little work but your tastebuds are rewarded with a tantalising soup that is great at any time of the year.

MUSHROOM SOUP

SERVES: 1
COOKING TIME: 4 minutes,
  plus 10 minutes
  steeping (if not steep-
  ing overnight)
EQUIPMENT: 300ml/½ pint
  mug, additional mug
  or bowl

6g/¼oz dried mushrooms
125ml/4½fl oz/½ cup water,
  just-boiled
50g/1¾oz button/white
  mushrooms, finely
  chopped

15ml/1 tbsp onion, finely
  diced
½ clove garlic, finely
  chopped
7.5ml/1½ tsp butter
2 fresh sage leaves, finely
  sliced
60ml/4 tbsp wholemeal/
  whole-wheat breadcrumbs
90ml/3fl oz/generous ⅓ cup
  stock
15ml/1 tbsp double/heavy
  cream
Seasoning

1 Put the dried mushrooms in a mug or bowl and steep in the just-boiled water for at least 10 minutes (you can make this the night before and leave it in the refrigerator overnight).

2 Add the diced button mushrooms to another mug with the onion, garlic, butter, sage leaves and seasoning and microwave covered for 2 minutes.

3 Remove the rehydrated mushrooms, squeezing out their excess liquid (keep the liquid, you will use it in the soup).

4 Finely chop the rehydrated mushrooms and add to the rest of the cooked ingredients along with the breadcrumbs and two-thirds of the stock. Cover and microwave for 1½ minutes.

5 Add the reserved liquid (there should be about 60ml/4 tbsp) and the remaining stock to the mug and microwave for a final 30 seconds to warm through.

6 Finish with a tablespoon of cream.

CHEF'S NOTES:
There is usually a little sediment at the bottom of the mushroom stock from the dried mushrooms, you can avoid pouring this into the soup by passing it through a sieve or strainer if you prefer.
  For an extra-indulgent soup add a few drops of brandy at the end!

This soup is based on an old Greek favourite. It's a warming, creamy soup with a little sharpness due to the yogurt. But it's really the chunks of just-melting Halloumi cheese that keep me coming back for more.

TRAHANA — BULGUR WHEAT AND YOGURT SOUP

1 Add the onion, garlic and olive oil to a mug with a pinch of seasoning and microwave covered for 1 minute.

2 Combine the bulgur wheat with the onion and garlic mixture and add a quarter of the stock (60ml/2fl oz/ ¼ cup) to the mug. Microwave covered for 2½ minutes.

3 Add 120ml/4fl oz/½ cup of the stock, stir and microwave covered for a further 2½ minutes.

4 Finally add the Halloumi cheese, yogurt, and the remaining stock (enough to fill the mug or to your preference) and microwave uncovered for 30 seconds to warm through.

5 Garnish with lemon wedges and lots of black pepper.

CHEF'S TIPS:
Try adding a pinch of dried oregano or thyme for a slightly different flavour.

SERVES: **1**
COOKING TIME: **6½ minutes**
EQUIPMENT: **300ml/½ pint mug**

15ml/1 tbsp onion, diced
½ clove garlic, diced
7.5ml/1½ tsp olive oil
30g/1oz bulgur wheat, rinsed

240ml/8fl oz/1 cup stock
20g/¾oz Halloumi cheese, diced
30ml/2 tbsp Greek/US strained plain yogurt
Lemon wedges and black pepper, to garnish
Seasoning

Sweet potato, coconut and ginger are great friends and combining them creates a fiery and creamy soup in one go. Delicious on its own it can also act as a base for a myriad of other ingredients including shellfish, chicken or even aubergine.

FIERY SWEET POTATO AND COCONUT SOUP

SERVES: 1
COOKING TIME: 7–7½ minutes
EQUIPMENT: 300ml/½ pint mug, additional mug or bowl

100g/3¾oz sweet potato, diced
90ml/6 tbsp tepid water
Pinch of salt
½ clove garlic, chopped
5ml/1 tsp chopped fresh red chilli
10ml/2 tsp fresh root ginger, grated
7.5ml/1½ tsp olive oil
2.5ml/½ tsp cumin seeds
1.5ml/¼ tsp ground cumin
1.5ml/¼ tsp ground coriander
100ml/3½fl oz/scant ½ cup coconut milk
30ml/2 tbsp stock (optional)
Fresh coriander/cilantro sprigs, to garnish

1 Add the sweet potato to a mug or bowl with the water and a pinch of salt, and microwave uncovered for 5 minutes (place the mug on a plate for any overspills) and reserve.

2 In a separate mug, add the garlic, chilli, ginger, olive oil and spices, and microwave uncovered for 1 minute.

3 Drain the sweet potato and mash with the back of a fork as much as possible before combining with the cooked aromatics. Add the coconut milk and stock, if you want it looser, and microwave for 1 minute to warm through; microwave for an extra 30 seconds if not hot enough. Garnish with coriander sprigs.

CHEF'S NOTES:
I love ginger and you'll really taste it in this recipe which also adds a little heat; feel free to add less and reduce the chilli if you don't want it too hot.
    This soup is great with prawns/shrimp as well!

Packed with root vegetables and wrapped lovingly in a warm spiced broth, this is a nice take on a traditional vegetable soup and filling enough to keep you going.

RUSTIC VEGETABLE SPICED SOUP

1 Add all the ingredients to a mug except the celery leaves and using only 60ml/4 tbsp stock. Microwave, covered, for 5 minutes (put the mug on a plate to catch any overspill).

2 Add another 30ml/2 tbsp of stock to the mug and microwave covered for a further 3 minutes.

3 Finish by topping up the mug with the remaining stock and microwave for 30 seconds if not hot enough.

4 Garnish with chopped fresh celery leaves.

CHEF'S NOTES:
You can swap the celery leaves for parsley.
   Substitute any root vegetables as you prefer; parsnips work very well!

SERVES: **1**
COOKING TIME: **8–8½ minutes**
EQUIPMENT: **300ml/½ pint mug**

10g/⅓oz onion, finely diced
10g/⅓oz celery, finely diced
10g/⅓oz leek, finely diced
15g/½oz carrot, finely diced
25g/1oz potato, finely diced
25g/1oz fresh or frozen peas
½ clove garlic, finely
   chopped

7.5ml/1½ tsp olive oil
125ml/4fl oz/½ cup chopped
   canned tomatoes
2.5ml/½ tsp turmeric
1.5ml/¼ tsp nigella seeds
Pinch of cayenne pepper
Pinch of ground cumin
180ml/6fl oz/¾ cup stock
Fresh celery leaves, chopped,
   to garnish
Seasoning

Sweet potato cooks really well in the microwave and the combination with earthy, fragrant rosemary is wonderfully warming. It sounds like a grown-up soup but the youngest in our family enjoyed it too!

SWEET POTATO AND ROSEMARY SOUP

1 Add the spring onion, garlic and olive oil to a mug and microwave uncovered for 1 minute.

2 Then add the sweet potato, seasoning and 60ml/ 4 tbsp stock. Place the mug on a plate to catch any overspill and microwave uncovered for 5 minutes.

3 Mash the sweet potato mixture as much as possible with the back of a fork before adding the flour and combining thoroughly. Add the butter, rosemary, smoked paprika and the remaining stock.

4 Place the mug back on the plate and microwave again for 2 minutes uncovered. Top with extra stock, if required.

CHEF'S NOTES:
Ensure you chop up the rosemary leaves as fine as possible and avoid any stalks.
   Add a spoonful of thick cream for a richer and more silky texture.

SERVES: 1
COOKING TIME: 8 minutes
EQUIPMENT: 300ml/½ pint
   mug

1 spring onion/scallion, sliced
1 clove garlic, diced
5ml/1 tsp olive oil
70g/2½oz sweet potato,
   diced
185ml/6fl oz/¾ cup stock,
   plus a little extra if needed
10ml/2 tsp flour
10ml/2 tsp butter
A couple of sprigs fresh
   rosemary, leaves only
   finely chopped (see
   chef's notes)
Pinch of smoked paprika
Seasoning

Simplicity itself but oh so comforting. The warm umami flavours of Asia in a delicate miso broth with floating clouds of tofu, created in just 2 minutes.

MISO AND TOFU BROTH

SERVES: **1**
COOKING TIME: **2 minutes**
EQUIPMENT: **300ml/½ pint mug**

1 spring onion/scallion, sliced, plus extra to garnish
½ clove garlic, finely chopped
5ml/1 tsp fresh root ginger, grated
5g/¼oz kale, shredded, stalks removed
2.5ml/½ tsp sesame oil
100ml/3½fl oz/scant ½ cup stock
40g/1½oz tofu, diced
7.5ml/1½ tsp miso paste
2.5ml/½ tsp light soy sauce
Red chilli, sliced to garnish
Seasoning

1 Add the spring onion, garlic, ginger, kale, sesame oil and seasoning to a mug and microwave uncovered for 1 minute.

2 Now add the stock, tofu, miso paste and soy sauce and microwave for a further minute uncovered.

3 Garnish with extra spring onion and red chilli slices.

CHEF'S NOTES:
Miso paste can vary in strength and flavour; use just 7.5ml/1½ tsp at first and then taste, adding more if preferred.
   You can swap the kale for dried seaweed if you happen to have some, or savoy cabbage.

Seductively red with fresh beetroot: my quick Borscht has a beautiful contrast of deep red with a white swirl of sour cream. Earthy with a hint of sharpness, this lively soup is perfect for any time of year.

BORSCHT — BEETROOT AND SOUR CREAM SOUP

1 Add the garlic, spring onion, olive oil, celery, leek, carrot, beetroot, tomato, seasoning and 30ml/2 tbsp stock to a mug, combine thoroughly and microwave, covered, for 3 minutes.

2 Add the cornflour, mix thoroughly, followed by the cumin and remaining stock (to just fill) and microwave uncovered for 1 minute.

3 Add the vinegar to taste and garnish with dill, sour cream and a pinch of nigella seeds.

CHEF'S NOTES:
Try adding some shredded cabbage at the start for a heartier meal.

SERVES: 1
COOKING TIME: 4 minutes
EQUIPMENT: 300ml/½ pint
   mug

½ clove garlic, sliced
½ spring onion/scallion,
   sliced
7.5ml/1½ tsp olive oil
6g/¼oz celery, diced
6g/¼oz leek, diced
6g/¼oz carrot, diced
25g/1oz fresh beetroot/beet,
   peeled and grated
1 cherry tomato, about
   15ml/1 tbsp, diced
250ml/8½fl oz/1 cup stock
7.5ml/1½ tsp cornflour/
   cornstarch
Pinch of ground cumin
2.5ml/½ tsp balsamic vinegar
Fresh dill, sour cream and
   pinch of nigella seeds,
   to garnish
Seasoning

As soon as I started writing this recipe book I knew I wanted to create a pear, walnut and blue cheese soup. The ingredients work incredibly well, with a delicate balance of flavours, and this is one of the more 'grown-up' soups.

PEAR, WALNUT AND BLUE CHEESE SOUP

1 Add the potato, pear, walnuts, milk, 60ml/4 tbsp stock and seasoning to a mug, cover and microwave for 6 minutes. Place the mug on a plate to catch any overspill. Pour away any overspill.

2 Mash the mixture as much as possible with a fork before adding the flour. Combine the flour fully before adding the remaining stock and butter. Microwave uncovered for 2 minutes.

3 Finally stir in the blue cheese and season generously with black pepper. Garnish with a few cubes of diced pear, walnuts and a couple of clumps of blue cheese.

CHEF'S NOTES:
Add a splash of cream for an extra rich and indulgent soup.
   A lovely creamy Dolcelatte was used here but if you prefer a stronger blue cheese swap for a Gorgonzola, Stilton or similar.

SERVES: 1
COOKING TIME: 8 minutes
EQUIPMENT: 300ml/½ pint mug

50g/2oz potato, diced
85g/3oz pear, diced, plus extra to garnish
15g/½oz walnuts, chopped, plus extra to garnish
15ml/1 tbsp milk
180ml/6fl oz/¾ cup stock
7.5ml/1½ tsp plain/ all-purpose flour
5ml/1 tsp butter
20g/¾oz creamy blue cheese, preferably Dolcelatte, plus extra to garnish
Seasoning

Warming spices combined with little pockets of sweetness from the apricot keep you coming back for more of this one. The chickpeas give a nice texture to the soup whilst also making it filling enough to get you through the day. If you don't have apricots you can use pretty much any other dried sweet fruit.

MOROCCAN CHICKPEA AND APRICOT SOUP

SERVES: 1
COOKING TIME: 4½ minutes
EQUIPMENT: 300ml/½ pint mug

5g/¼oz onion, finely diced
5g/¼oz carrot, finely diced
5g/¼oz celery, finely diced
5g/¼oz leek, finely diced
½ clove garlic, finely chopped
7.5ml/1½ tsp olive oil
1.5ml/¼ tsp ground cumin
1.5ml/¼ tsp ground cinnamon, plus a pinch to garnish

1.5ml/¼ tsp ground coriander
2.5ml/½ tsp ground smoked paprika
100g/3¾oz canned chickpeas
5ml/1 tsp tomato purée
150ml/5fl oz/⅔ cup stock
2.5ml/½ tsp honey
5g/¼oz ready-to-eat dried apricot, diced
A couple of sprigs fresh coriander/cilantro, finely chopped
Seasoning

1 Add the onion, carrot, celery, leek, garlic and olive oil into a mug and microwave covered for 1 minute.

2 Add all the spices and seasoning, and microwave covered for a further 1 minute.

3 Now add the chickpeas, tomato purée and 60ml/ 4 tbsp of the stock and microwave, covered, for 2 minutes.

4 Lightly mash with the back of a fork to help break up some of the chickpeas before adding the honey, remaining stock and diced apricot. Microwave uncovered for 30 seconds to warm through.

5 Garnish with a pinch of cinnamon and some chopped fresh coriander.

CHEF'S NOTES:
This makes a lovely vegetarian soup, however, you could add some diced chicken at the start for a meatier version and even some cayenne pepper for some warmth.

A nice take on the classic carrot and coriander soup, butternut squash gives a lovely sweet and nutty flavour that complements the freshness of the coriander perfectly. It is also a brilliant base to add other ingredients that you may have left over.

BUTTERNUT SQUASH AND CORIANDER SOUP

1 Add the spring onion, garlic and olive oil to a mug and microwave uncovered for 1 minute.

2 Add the butternut squash, 60ml/4 tbsp stock and seasoning before microwaving, covered, for 5 minutes.

3 Once cooked, mash with the back of a fork as much as possible, add the remaining stock, cumin, cornflour and milk, and microwave uncovered for 1 minute.

4 Mix through the chopped coriander and rest for a minute. Garnish with a sprig.

CHEF'S NOTES:
If you prefer a looser soup halve the amount of cornflour used.

You can also replace the coriander with fresh thyme for an earthier version.

If you have leftover roasted butternut squash it makes for a much richer depth of flavour.

Add a little diced smoked bacon or a dash of cream.

SERVES: 1
COOKING TIME: 7 minutes, plus 1 minute resting
EQUIPMENT: 300ml/½ pint mug

½ spring onion/scallion, sliced
½ clove garlic, finely chopped
15ml/1 tbsp olive oil
100g/3¾oz butternut squash, diced
160ml/5½fl oz/⅔ cup stock
1.5ml/¼ tsp ground cumin
10ml/2 tsp cornflour/cornstarch
15ml/1 tbsp milk
15ml/1 tbsp chopped fresh coriander/cilantro, plus a sprig to garnish
Seasoning

One of my favourites soups, with the cream cheese complementing the subtlety of the asparagus. I like to give a little swirl of olive oil at the end to make it look pretty.

ASPARAGUS AND CREAM CHEESE SOUP

1 Add the spring onion, garlic and olive oil to a mug and microwave uncovered for 1 minute.

2 Add the asparagus and 60ml/4 tbsp stock before microwaving, covered, for 5 minutes.

3 Once cooked mash with the back of a fork as much as possible, add the remaining stock, seasoning and cornflour, and microwave uncovered for 90 seconds.

4 Add the cream cheese and stir through until melted and season again.

CHEF'S NOTES:
You can vary the thickness of the soup by slightly increasing or decreasing the amount of cornflour used.
  If you need a carnivorous fix a little diced smoked bacon or chicken added at the start goes really well with this soup.

SERVES: 1
COOKING TIME: **7½ minutes**
EQUIPMENT: **300ml/½ pint mug**

½ spring onion/scallion, sliced
½ clove garlic, finely chopped
5ml/1 tsp olive oil
60g/2¼oz asparagus, finely chopped
250ml/8fl oz/1 cup stock
7.5ml/1½ tsp cornflour/ cornstarch
7.5ml/1½ tsp cream cheese
Seasoning

SPEEDY SEAFOOD SOUPS

Seafood and microwaves are great friends. The delicate structure of fish and seafood means it cooks brilliantly in the microwave and always remains succulent and packed with flavour. Seafood is also extremely quick – the best ingredient for this fast, fun and fabulous collection of soups! You can also swap the seafood for diced chicken if preferred as chicken cooks nearly as quickly as seafood.

There is something about a smoky haddock and cheese chowder that just shouts comfort food. This deliciously rich and cosy soup is perfect to curl up around on a cold winter's day.

SMOKED HADDOCK CHOWDER

1 Add the potato, pancetta or bacon, butter and half the stock to a mug and microwave, covered, for 4 minutes.

2 Once done, mash the potato with the back of a fork.

3 Add the milk and the remaining stock to the cooked potatoes and stir through before adding the haddock and smoked cheese.

4 Microwave uncovered for 2 minutes, then let stand for a minute before garnishing with the parsley and lots of black pepper.

CHEF'S NOTES:
If you can't find smoked cheese you can substitute a regular hard/medium cheese, such as Cheddar.

Try adding half a teaspoon of English mustard for extra flavour and a little heat.

If you want an even thicker soup, add more potato at the start.

SERVES: **1**
COOKING TIME: **6 minutes, plus 1 minute standing**
EQUIPMENT: **300ml/½ pint mug**

80g/3oz potato, diced into roughly 1cm/½in cubes
20g/¾oz smoked pancetta (or streaky/fatty bacon), cubed

15ml/1 tbsp butter
120ml/4fl oz/½ cup stock
30ml/2 tbsp milk
65g/2½oz smoked undyed haddock, cubed
15g/½oz smoked cheese, grated
Finely chopped fresh parsley, to garnish
Seasoning

Cambodia is a country unlike any other, full of contrasts. This soup is reminiscent of a dish I enjoyed in Battambang; having a history of French colonisation, a baguette served on the side wouldn't be unheard of!

CAMBODIAN SEAFOOD SOUP

SERVES: 1
COOKING TIME: 2½ minutes
EQUIPMENT: 300ml/½ pint
   mug

½ spring onion/scallion,
   sliced
7.5ml/1½ tsp olive oil
5ml/1 tsp chopped fresh
   green chilli
2.5ml/½ tsp garlic, minced/
   ground
7.5ml/1½ tsp fresh root
   ginger, grated
70g/2¾oz mixed seafood
250ml/8fl oz/1 cup stock
2.5ml/½ tsp light soy sauce
2.5ml/½ tsp fish sauce
2.5ml/½ tsp honey
Pinch of salt
7.5ml/1½ tsp lime juice

1 Add the spring onion, olive oil, chilli, garlic and ginger and microwave covered for 1 minute.

2 Add the seafood, half the stock, the soy sauce, fish sauce, honey and salt and microwave again for 90 seconds.

3 Top with any more stock, as preferred, and serve with lime juice.

CHEF'S NOTES:
I use the frozen mixed seafood (prawns/shrimp, cockles, scallops and squid rings) for convenience.

Saganaki translates to the small pan that is usually used in Cyprus to cook the dish. Traditionally a saganaki is quite a thick dish, but the flavours are divine and work wonderfully together to create a soup. Prawns, feta, tomatoes, a dash of ouzo – what's not to like!

PRAWN SAGANAKI SOUP

1 Add the garlic, spring onion, olive oil, seasoning, smoked paprika and chilli flakes to a mug, combine and microwave, uncovered for 30 seconds.

2 Add the passata, stock, prawns and ouzo to the mug and, once combined, microwave uncovered for 2 minutes.

3 Add a pinch of sugar to taste, and stir through the chopped parsley. Crumble the feta cheese on top and garnish with extra parsley.

CHEF'S NOTES:
You can always replace the ouzo with a dash of white wine if more convenient (or leave out the alcohol).

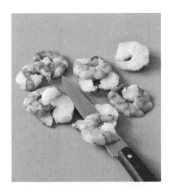 

SERVES: 1
COOKING TIME: 2½ minutes
EQUIPMENT: 300ml/½ pint
    mug

½ clove garlic, minced/
    ground
½ spring onion/scallion,
    sliced
7.5ml/1½ tsp extra virgin
    olive oil
2.5ml/½ tsp smoked paprika
Pinch of chilli flakes

60ml/2fl oz/¼ cup passata/
    bottled strained tomatoes
90ml/3fl oz/¾ cup stock
50g/2oz king prawns/jumbo
    shrimp, cut in half
7.5ml/1½ tsp ouzo
Pinch of sugar
15ml/1 tbsp chopped
    fresh parsley, plus extra
    to garnish
20g/¾oz feta cheese,
    crumbled
Seasoning

Such fresh vibrant ingredients, the addition of turmeric gives this soup a subtle earthy note and a beautiful golden colour. One of my favourite soups and perfect for warming the soul.

SALMON AND TURMERIC SOUP

SERVES: 1
COOKING TIME: 1 minute 45 seconds
EQUIPMENT: 300ml/½ pint mug

1 spring onion/scallion, sliced
2.5cm/1in fresh root ginger, cut into julienne strips
½ lemon grass stalk, finely chopped
1.5ml/¼ tsp ground turmeric
5ml/1 tsp olive oil
5ml/1 tsp sesame oil
Pinch of dried chilli flakes
100g/3¾oz salmon, roughly cut into 2.5cm/1in squares
185ml/6½fl oz/generous ¾ cup stock
5ml/1 tsp lime juice
Fresh coriander/cilantro sprigs, to garnish

1 Combine all the ingredients except the stock, lime juice and coriander in a mug and microwave covered for 1 minute.

2 Add the stock and lime juice, gently combine the ingredients and microwave uncovered for 45 seconds.

3 Garnish with the fresh herb.

CHEF'S NOTES:
If you are using hot stock then you may not need to microwave for a second time.

If you don't want your soup to be too hot (chilli heat) you can leave out the chilli altogether or sprinkle at the end of cooking so you have pockets of heat as opposed to the whole soup being the same level of spiciness.

A Greek fisherman's soup is humble in its origins. The leftover fish from the day's catch is cooked on deck, for a hearty and clean-tasting broth filled with pieces of different fish.

GREEK FISHERMAN'S SOUP

1 Add the onion, garlic, tomatoes, olive oil and seasoning to a mug and microwave uncovered for 2 minutes.

2 Then add the fish, stock and oregano, and microwave again for 2 minutes uncovered.

3 Garnish with a small squeeze of lemon juice and chopped fresh parsley.

CHEF'S NOTES:

In true keeping with a Greek Fisherman's Soup you can use whatever fish you want including salmon, cod, haddock, prawns/shrimp, etc. The main thing is to cube them all about the same size so they cook evenly.

To save money you can buy small pieces of fish from the deli counter at your local supermarket (or just save a few offcuts and freeze them until you have enough!).

Try adding fresh dill instead of parsley for a more anise-flavoured dish.

SERVES: **1**
COOKING TIME: **4 minutes**
EQUIPMENT: **300ml/½ pint mug**

10g/⅓oz onion, diced
1 clove garlic, sliced
50ml/2fl oz/¼ cup fresh tomatoes, chopped
15ml/1 tbsp olive oil
100g/3¾oz fish, diced roughly into 2.5cm/1in cubes
90ml/3fl oz/¾ cup stock
Pinch of dried oregano
Lemon juice and chopped fresh parsley, to garnish
Seasoning

A delicate and wholesome prawn and rice noodle soup with a slight hint of Asian flavours. The fresh mint, coriander and lime juice added at the end of cooking give a vibrant and cleansing punch. Perfect when you want something that tastes as healthy as it is.

CLEANSING PRAWN NOODLE SOUP

1 First cook the noodles by submerging them in just-boiled water and leaving for 5 minutes (you can also microwave them for 3 minutes).

2 Once the noodles are just cooked put them in a mug with the celery, garlic, olive oil, prawns, stock and spinach or pak choi, and microwave uncovered for 1½ minutes.

3 Mix through a couple of good pinches of fresh coriander and mint and finally the lime juice.

4 Let stand for a minute before consuming.

CHEF'S NOTES:
You can swap the prawns for other fish but the prawns keep the broth really clean and add a nice little crunch to the soup.

SERVES: 1
COOKING TIME: 4½–6½ minutes, plus **1** minute standing
EQUIPMENT: 300ml/½ pint mug

30g/1oz rice noodles
10g/⅓oz celery, thinly sliced
1 clove garlic, diced
15ml/1 tbsp olive oil
60g/2oz king prawns/jumbo shrimp, halved lengthways
60ml/2fl oz/¼ cup stock
10g/⅓oz spinach or pak choi/ bok choy, roughly cut
15ml/1 tbsp chopped fresh coriander/cilantro
15ml/1 tbsp chopped fresh mint
7.5ml/1½ tsp lime juice

Seriously, wow. This is good, the dill blends into the cream and complements the salmon perfectly. The fish gives this delicate soup a hearty punch.

SALMON AND DILL CREAM SOUP

SERVES: 1
COOKING TIME: **4 minutes,**
   plus 1 minute resting
EQUIPMENT: **300ml/½ pint**
   mug

½ clove garlic, diced
1 spring onion/scallion, sliced
   (white part only)
15g/½oz leek, sliced
7.5ml/1½ tsp butter

80g/3oz salmon, diced
   roughly into 2.5cm/
   1in cubes
A couple of sprigs chopped
   fresh dill, plus extra to
   garnish
125ml/4fl oz/½ cup stock,
   plus extra if needed
5ml/1 tsp cornflour/
   cornstarch
15ml/1 tbsp double/heavy
   cream
Seasoning

1 Add the garlic, spring onion, leek and butter to a mug and microwave uncovered for 2 minutes.

2 Then add the cubed salmon, dill, stock and cornflour, and microwave uncovered for a further 2 minutes.

3 Gently stir to help break up the salmon and rest for a minute before finishing with the cream and topping up with stock if necessary.

4 Garnish with extra fresh dill and season to taste.

CHEF'S NOTES:
Add another teaspoon of cornflour if you prefer a thicker soup.
   If you prefer to avoid cream you can replace with milk for a lighter version (but it won't be quite as indulgent!).

Thai green curry is famous the world over and this slightly looser version makes the perfect mug soup meal. The aromatics give an enticing flavour that almost guarantees you'll be coming back again and again. Feel free to omit the prawns for vegetables or even chicken or pork.

GREEN THAI CURRY PRAWN SOUP

SERVES: **1**
COOKING TIME: **3–4 minutes**
EQUIPMENT: **300ml/½ pint mug**

1 clove garlic, grated
7.5ml/1½ tsp fresh root ginger, grated
7.5ml/1½ tsp fresh lemon grass, finely chopped
5ml/1 tsp chopped fresh green chilli
7.5ml/1½ tsp olive oil
1 spring onion/scallion, sliced
10g/⅓oz fine green bean, cut into four
15g/½oz finely chopped (including stalks) fresh coriander/cilantro
2.5ml/½ tsp cornflour/cornstarch
40g/1½oz king prawns/jumbo shrimp, deveined and shelled (about 5 depending on size)
10g/⅓oz vermicelli rice noodles
90ml/3fl oz/¾ cup stock
60ml/2fl oz/¼ cup coconut milk
5ml/1 tsp fish sauce
5ml/1 tsp lime juice
Pinch of brown sugar
Pinch of salt
Lime zest, to garnish

1 Add the garlic, ginger, lemon grass, chilli and olive oil to a mug and microwave uncovered for 1 minute.

2 Add the spring onion, green bean, coriander and cornflour to the mug, and mix well before adding the prawns, rice noodles and finally the stock. Microwave covered for 2 minutes.

3 Finally add the rest of the ingredients and warm through in the microwave for 30 seconds or more if needed.

4 Garnish with a few grates of lime zest.

CHEF'S NOTES:
Try adding a medley of seafood including sliced baby squid and mussels, or opt for a vegetarian version by replacing the shellfish with mangetouts/snow peas and baby corn.

If you want more of a chilli kick use a small green bird's eye chilli instead – but be warned it can be very, very hot!

Inspired by Jambalaya, this symbolises everything I love about Louisiana; a true melting pot of French, Spanish and American cultures. Every household has their own version, slow-cooked for the whole family. This is my soupy rice-free version, cooked in minutes.

SLOPPY JAMBALAYA

SERVES: 1
COOKING TIME: 5½ minutes
EQUIPMENT: 300ml/½ pint mug

½ spring onion/scallion, sliced
15ml/1 tbsp celery, diced
15ml/1 tbsp red bell pepper, diced
15ml/1 tbsp green bell pepper, diced
15ml/1 tbsp yellow bell pepper, diced
1 clove garlic, finely chopped
10g/⅓oz/about 2 okra, sliced
2.5ml/½ tsp fresh oregano
2 sprigs of fresh thyme, leaves only
5ml/1 tsp chopped green jalapeño chilli
Pinch of cayenne pepper
Pinch of ground cumin
2.5ml/½ tsp smoked paprika
1.5ml/¼ tsp ground coriander
15ml/1 tbsp olive oil
40g/1½oz/about 6 king prawns/jumbo shrimp
7.5ml/1½ tsp plain/ all-purpose flour
7.5ml/1½ tsp tomato purée
150ml/5fl oz/⅔ cup stock
2.5ml/½ tsp vinegar
Fresh parsley or coriander/ cilantro sprigs, to garnish
Seasoning

1 Add the spring onion, celery, peppers, garlic, okra, oregano, thyme, seasoning, chilli, all the spices and olive oil to a mug and microwave covered for 3 minutes.

2 Now add the prawns and flour, and mix well before adding the tomato purée, stock and vinegar, and mix again. Microwave uncovered for 90 seconds, stir and continue microwaving for a further minute.

3 Garnish with parsley or coriander sprigs.

CHEF'S NOTES:
Add a few slices of smoked sausage as well (traditionally Andouille sausage would be used).
   If you prefer a vegetarian version, omit the prawns and double the quantity of okra.

CHICKEN SOUPS

Poultry is extremely versatile and has a flavour that marries with other ingredients really well, giving you almost endless choices and combinations. Chicken cooked in the microwave comes out succulent and tasty, and is surprisingly quick to cook, making it a great ingredient to use for soups.

It doesn't get much more classic or universal than a good old chicken noodle soup! Simplicity itself, but don't let that fool you; this never fails to satisfy.

CHICKEN NOODLE SOUP

SERVES: 1
COOKING TIME: 6½ minutes,
   plus 1 minute standing
EQUIPMENT: 300ml/½ pint
   mug

20g/¾oz medium dried egg
   noodles
250ml/8fl oz/1 cup just-boiled
   water

Pinch of salt
5g/¼oz carrot, finely diced
5g/¼oz celery, finely diced
20g/¾oz chicken breast,
   finely diced
125ml/4fl oz/½ cup stock
Chopped fresh parsley, to
   garnish
Ground black pepper

1 Break up the egg noodles and place in a mug with the just-boiled water and a good pinch of salt. Place the mug on a plate to catch the overspill and microwave uncovered for 4 minutes.

2 Drain the noodles and add the rest of the ingredients; combine well and microwave uncovered for 2½ minutes. Let stand for a minute.

3 Garnish with chopped fresh parsley and season with black pepper to taste.

CHEF'S NOTES:
This is a great recipe to use up leftover chicken. If you are using pre-cooked chicken you can reduce the cooking time by half.
   You can also use fresh egg noodles that cook in about a minute to save even more time.

My mum might not speak to me again after reading this microwave recipe! Avgolemoni is a staple of Cypriot cooking; a deliciously warming and zesty chicken soup with the addition of lemon and an egg giving the soup a rich creaminess.

AVGOLEMONI — GREEK CHICKEN SOUP

1 Add the diced chicken breast and stock to a mug or bowl and microwave uncovered for 1½ minutes (or until the chicken is cooked).

2 In a separate mug add the lemon juice and cornflour and stir until fully combined, then pour the cornflour mixture into the mug with the cooked chicken and stock and stir.

3 Using the mug that had the cornflour mixture in, crack an egg and whisk, then pour half the egg mixture into the soup and gently stir twice.

4 Microwave uncovered for 30 seconds, and season.

CHEF'S NOTES:
You can save the leftover egg mixture to use the next day (covered in the refrigerator) or make another mug soup for your friend!

The final soup will almost look like an egg drop soup with little slithers of egg running through it; taste for more lemon or black pepper.

If you want to make this a heartier soup you can add some cooked rice or pasta to it at the start.

SERVES: 1
COOKING TIME: 2–3 minutes
EQUIPMENT: 300ml/½ pint mug, additional mug or bowl

80g/3oz chicken breast, diced roughly into 1cm/ ½in cubes

185ml/6½fl oz/generous ¾ cup stock

15ml/1 tbsp lemon juice

7.5ml/1½ tsp cornflour/ cornstarch

1 egg

Seasoning (heavy on the black pepper)

Laksa is a delicate and fragrant soup which is part of the Peranakan cuisine – literally a melting pot of both Chinese and Malay cuisines. This isn't just a soup; it is a beautifully balanced dish that is perfect with fish, meat or vegetables.

RED CHICKEN LAKSA

SERVES: 1
COOKING TIME: 4½–5 minutes
EQUIPMENT: 300ml/½ pint
   mug

1 clove garlic, grated
2.5cm/1in piece fresh root
   ginger, grated
5ml/1 tsp finely chopped
   fresh lemon grass
5ml/1 tsp chopped fresh
   red chilli
15ml/1 tbsp olive oil
½ spring onion/scallion,
   sliced
2.5ml/½ tsp tomato purée
1 button/white mushroom
   (approx. 12g/½oz), sliced

30g/1oz chicken breast,
   diced
2.5ml/½ tsp cornflour/
   cornstarch
2.5ml/½ tsp paprika
10g/⅓oz vermicelli rice
   noodles
90ml/3fl oz/scant ½ cup stock
90ml/3fl oz/scant ½ cup
   coconut milk
5ml/1 tsp fish sauce
2.5ml/½ tsp honey or brown
   sugar
5ml/1 tsp lime juice
Seasoning

1 Add the garlic, ginger, lemon grass, chilli and olive oil to a mug and microwave uncovered for 1 minute.

2 Add the spring onion, tomato purée, mushroom, chicken, cornflour and paprika to the mug and stir thoroughly before adding the noodles and stock (you may need to break the noodles to fit in the mug!). Microwave, covered, for 3 minutes.

3 Finally, add the rest of the ingredients and warm through in the microwave for 30 seconds, or more if needed.

CHEF'S NOTES:
Delicious as it is, if you prefer a vegetarian version swap the chicken breast for new potato chunks or baby aubergines/eggplants.
   I've used jalapeño chillies for a medium heat. However, when travelling through Asia quite often the smaller (and drastically hotter) bird's eye chillies would be used – use at your own peril!

I don't know anyone who doesn't love a decent ramen noodle soup – and if I did I would have to disown them immediately! My version comes complete with a boiled egg cooked in the microwave as well.

CHICKEN RAMEN

1 Add the salt to a mug or bowl and fill with the tepid water. Stir until the salt is dissolved then add the egg (in its shell), along with the broken rice noodles.

2 Microwave uncovered for 4 minutes, then pour the hot water away and rinse with cold water a couple of times.

3 Drain fully (I use a fork and just tip the water out), remove the whole egg and set aside, and add a drizzle of sesame oil over the noodles to stop them sticking.

4 In a separate mug combine the teaspoon of sesame oil, spring onion, garlic, ginger and olive oil, and microwave uncovered for 1 minute.

5 Once done, add the noodles, chicken, mushroom, stock, honey, soy sauce, pak choi and a pinch of salt to the mug and microwave uncovered for 2 minutes.

6 Peel the boiled egg and cut in half, place on top of the soup and garnish with the chilli and coriander.

CHEF'S NOTES:
You must add salt when boiling the egg otherwise it will explode! Most of the salt is not consumed as it is poured away with the cooking water.

Cooking time for a soft-boiled egg (when cooked with the noodles) does vary depending on the size of your egg, ambient temperature etc, but 4 minutes is about right.

I like to put the chicken, pak choi and mushrooms into the mug in groups rather than mixed all together.

Try adding more soy sauce to taste or a little squeeze of lime juice at the end.

SERVES: 1
COOKING TIME: 7 minutes
EQUIPMENT: 300ml/½ pint mug, additional mug or bowl

2.5ml/½ tsp salt
250ml/8fl oz/1 cup tepid water
1 medium/US large egg
20g/¾oz thin rice noodles, broken up
2.5ml/½ tsp sesame oil, plus an extra drizzle
1 spring onion/scallion, sliced
½ clove garlic, sliced
7.5ml/1½ tsp fresh root ginger, grated
2.5ml/½ tsp olive oil
40g/1½oz chicken breast, sliced 1cm/½in thick
20g/¾oz shiitake or button/white mushroom, sliced
100ml/3½fl oz/scant ½ cup stock
10ml/2 tsp honey
7.5ml/1½ tsp light soy sauce
30g/1oz/about 3 leaves pak choi/bok choy, sliced lengthways
Pinch of salt
Fresh red chilli, sliced, and fresh coriander/cilantro, to garnish

Every culture has its own version of Jewish Penicillin; the cure-all comfort soup that deserves to be slurped slowly. With most of my soups you can play about with the ingredients to suit your own personal taste, but whatever you decide to change in this recipe, keep the dill – it's the signature ingredient!

JEWISH PENICILLIN WITH TURKEY MEATBALLS

1 First make your turkey meatballs – add all the meatball ingredients together in a bowl using your hands and then roll into five balls, each about the size of a large marble, and reserve.

2 Now for the soup; add all the soup ingredients together in a mug except the stock and microwave covered for 90 seconds.

3 Gently add the turkey meatballs to the mug with the stock, and microwave uncovered for 2 minutes.

4 Let the soup rest for a couple of minutes before serving.

CHEF'S NOTES:
You can swap the minced turkey for chicken if you like.

SERVES: **1**
COOKING TIME: **3½ minutes, plus 2 minutes resting**
EQUIPMENT: **300ml/½ pint mug, bowl**

½ spring onion/scallion, sliced
10g/⅓oz carrot, diced
5g/¼oz celery, diced
½ clove garlic, sliced
15ml/1 tbsp olive oil
185ml/6fl oz/generous ¾ cup stock
Seasoning

For the meatballs
7.5ml/1½ tsp chopped fresh parsley
7.5ml/1½ tsp chopped fresh dill
40g/1½oz minced/ground turkey
5ml/1 tsp olive oil
10g/⅓oz broken crackers
Seasoning

Allspice, Scotch bonnets and the holy trinity of spring onions, celery and bell peppers bring this soup alive, paying homage to the vibrant flavours of the Caribbean. A sure-fire winner to get your tastebuds dancing!

CARIBBEAN CHICKEN SOUP

SERVES: 1
COOKING TIME: 6 minutes,
plus 2 minutes standing
EQUIPMENT: 300ml/½ pint
mug

1 spring onion/scallion, sliced
1 clove garlic, diced
10g/⅓oz green bell pepper, diced
10g/⅓oz red bell pepper, diced
10g/⅓oz celery, diced
5g/¼oz carrot, diced
20g/¾oz/about 3 okra, sliced
2.5ml/½ tsp Scotch bonnet chilli, diced
3 fresh thyme sprigs (stalks removed)
1.5ml/¼ tsp allspice
15ml/1 tbsp olive oil
5ml/1 tsp tomato purée
50g/2oz chicken breast, thinly sliced
30g/1¼oz frozen peas
125ml/4fl oz/1 cup beef stock
7.5ml/1½ tsp orange juice
Fresh coriander sprigs, to garnish
Seasoning

1 Add the spring onion, garlic, peppers, celery, carrot, okra, chilli, thyme, allspice and olive oil to a mug and microwave covered for 3 minutes.

2 Add the tomato purée, chicken breast, peas, stock and orange juice, place the mug on a plate to catch any overspill, and microwave uncovered for 3 minutes.

3 Once cooked, let it stand for a couple of minutes before garnishing with fresh coriander sprigs and seasoning to taste.

CHEF'S NOTES:

Scotch bonnet chillies are hot! Wash your hands after chopping and try to not touch it too much.

If you want a more sweet and sour note add a few drops of vinegar and a pinch of sugar.

This soup is packed with flavour and makes a great vegetarian version – just swap the chicken for more okra or even diced courgettes/zucchini (and swap the beef stock for vegetable stock!).

This recipe is a total guilty pleasure for when I'm feeling exceptionally lazy and the kitchen cupboards are looking bare. In fact, this recipe would make the perfect student soup! It's quick and easy but delivers a decent chilli kick, is filling and is ideal for some instant soup gratification.

CHEAT'S HARISSA BAKED BEAN CHICKEN SOUP

1 Add all the ingredients to a mug and microwave uncovered for 3 minutes. Stir and then stand for a minute before microwaving again for 1 minute.

2 Rest for 2 minutes before devouring – if you have the patience – and garnish with some fresh coriander.

CHEF'S NOTES:
Swap the harissa paste for chipotle paste for a smokier and less hot version.

SERVES: 1
COOKING TIME: 4 minutes,
 plus 3 minutes standing
EQUIPMENT: 300ml/½ pint
 mug

125ml/4fl oz/½ cup canned
 baked beans
50g/2oz chicken breast,
 diced
1 spring onion/scallion, sliced
1.5ml/¼ tsp smoked paprika
1.5ml/¼ tsp ground cumin
5ml/1 tsp harissa paste
60ml/2fl oz/¼ cup stock
Fresh coriander/cilantro
 sprigs, to garnish

MAINLY MEATY SOUPS

Whether it be bacon, pork belly, minced lamb and even smoked sausages, these meats add a lovely depth of flavour to my microwave soups. When red meats are cooked in chunks they can get tough, so ensure they are submerged in the stock when being cooked. You can usually substitute red meats in these recipes for root vegetables if you want a vegetarian version.

Based on the traditional Polish soup consisting of garlic sausage and cabbage, this warming broth has a slight sharpness usually associated with sauerkraut, in this instance a dash of vinegar. It is perfect for warming the hands and heart of anyone that eats it.

KAPUSNIAK — POLISH SAUSAGE AND CABBAGE SOUP

SERVES: 1
COOKING TIME: 4½ minutes
EQUIPMENT: 300ml/½ pint
  mug

10g/⅓oz onion, finely diced
10g/⅓oz carrot, finely diced
15ml/1 tbsp smoked bacon,
  diced

40g/1½oz white cabbage, cut
  into 2.5cm/1in cubes
2.5ml/½ tsp white wine
  vinegar
30g/1¼oz Polish garlic
  sausage, diced chunky
Pinch of smoked paprika
90ml/3fl oz/scant ½ cup stock
5ml/1 tsp cornflour/
  cornstarch
5ml/1 tsp chopped fresh dill
Seasoning

1 Add the onion, carrot, bacon and cabbage to a mug and microwave, covered, for 3 minutes.

2 Add the rest of the ingredients except the dill and microwave uncovered for 1½ minutes.

3 Finish by stirring through the dill and an extra turn of black pepper.

CHEF'S NOTES:
A pinch of cayenne pepper works really well to add a little extra warmth.
  You can substitute malt vinegar for the white wine vinegar or even 2.5ml/½ tsp of Dijon mustard (stir through the mustard before adding the stock, to ensure it dissolves).

Bring a little Spanish sunshine to your meal with my chorizo and cannellini bean soup. Heating the chorizo at the start helps release its silky smoky oils into the rest of the soup and complements the creamy cannellini beans perfectly.

CHORIZO AND CANNELLINI BEAN SOUP

1 Add the chorizo, garlic, olive oil and tomato purée to a mug, mix thoroughly and microwave uncovered for 1 minute.

2 Add the passata, cannellini beans, sugar and seasoning and microwave uncovered for 1½ minutes. It will form a thick paste which is what you want.

3 Add the stock and mix thoroughly into the cooked paste, then microwave again if needed to warm through.

4 Stir through the chopped fresh coriander and garnish with a pinch of smoked paprika and a drizzle of extra virgin olive oil.

CHEF'S NOTES:
Try adding a small pinch of dried chilli flakes or cayenne pepper at the end if you like it spicy.
  Replace the coriander/cilantro with fresh basil or parsley for a slightly different flavour.

SERVES: 1
COOKING TIME: 2½–3 minutes
EQUIPMENT: 300ml/½ pint mug

30g/1¼oz chorizo, diced
½ clove garlic, chopped
7.5ml/1½ tsp olive oil
5ml/1 tsp tomato purée
60ml/2fl oz/¼ cup good-quality passata/bottled strained tomatoes
40g/1½oz canned cannellini beans
1.5ml/¼ tsp sugar
60ml/2fl oz/¼ cup stock
5ml/1 tsp chopped fresh coriander/cilantro
Pinch of smoked paprika and extra virgin olive oil, to garnish
Seasoning

Unbelievably quick and easy and a great twist on an old favourite.
Slightly sweet, spicy, sharp and sour, this soup will get the tastebuds
going into overdrive!

HOT AND SOUR SOUP

SERVES: 1
COOKING TIME: 1½ minutes
EQUIPMENT: 300ml/½ pint
    mug

30g/1¼oz smoked sausage
    or ham, sliced
30g/1¼oz fresh shiitake or
    button/white mushrooms,
    sliced

5ml/1 tsp light soy sauce
5ml/1 tsp honey
5ml/1 tsp fresh red chilli,
    sliced
7.5ml/1½ tsp rice wine
    vinegar (or malt vinegar but
    use slightly less)
½ spring onion/scallion,
    sliced
150ml/5fl oz/⅔ cup stock
5ml/1 tsp cornflour/
    cornstarch, mixed with
    5ml/1 tsp water
Pinch of salt

1 Combine all the ingredients and microwave
uncovered for 1½ minutes; stir gently after cooking.
That's it!

CHEF'S NOTES:
This can easily be transformed into a vegetarian
version by simply replacing the smoked sausage with
tofu and some more diced vegetables (carrots work
well!) and using vegetable stock.

   If you like a really thick hot and sour soup, increase
the quantity of cornflour.

'Hot Green' is the translation of the traditional Portuguese soup. Consisting of chorizo and spring greens (here I use savoy cabbage), this microwave mug soup is quick, fuss-free and perfect for a quick fix.

CALDO VERDE – PORTUGUESE CABBAGE SOUP

1 Add the chorizo, garlic, seasoning and olive oil to a mug and microwave uncovered for 30 seconds.

2 Add the potato, cabbage and half the stock, cover and microwave for 5 minutes.

3 Once done, break up the potatoes with the back of a fork, add the cornflour and remaining stock, or enough to fill the mug, and microwave uncovered for 1 minute.

CHEF'S NOTES:
Try a pinch of cayenne pepper to add some warmth. Substitute the savoy cabbage for kale or spring greens/collards.

SERVES: 1
COOKING TIME: 6½ minutes
EQUIPMENT: 300ml/½ pint
   mug

10g/⅓oz chorizo, diced
½ clove garlic, sliced
2.5ml/½ tsp olive oil

30g/1¼oz potato, diced
10g/⅓oz savoy cabbage,
   shredded
180ml/6½fl oz/generous ¾
   cup stock
5ml/1 tsp cornflour/
   cornstarch
Seasoning

This recipe is inspired by my travels through China, specifically the Chongqing area. Hot pots abound throughout China and South-east Asia, but for me it is the Szechuan hot pots, packed with a variety of chillies and the famous peppercorns, that I enjoy the most.

SZECHUAN HOT POT

1 Add the star anise, the sliced spring onion, salt, olive oil, fresh and dried chillies, Szechuan peppercorns, the spices, garlic, ginger and sesame oil to a mug, and microwave uncovered for 90 seconds.

2 Then add the rest of the ingredients except for the whole spring onion and watercress, and gently fold together in the mug. Before microwaving, trim the whole spring onion and place it vertically in the mug (so it looks like a straw). Microwave uncovered for 2 minutes.

3 Once done, rip the watercress into a couple of bunches and submerge in the soup and rest for a minute to let the watercress wilt (and remember not to eat the star anise – it's only for flavour!).

CHEF'S NOTES:
You can swap the rice wine vinegar for any other vinegar (but add less).

   If you don't have any Shaoxing rice wine the closest substitute is sherry.

SERVES: 1
COOKING TIME: 2½ minutes, plus 1 minute resting
EQUIPMENT: 300ml/½ pint mug

1 star anise, whole
15ml/1 tbsp spring onion/scallion, sliced, plus extra 1 whole
Pinch of salt
15ml/1 tbsp olive oil
5ml/1 tsp chopped fresh red chilli
Generous pinch of chilli flakes
1.5ml/¼ tsp Szechuan peppercorns, crushed
Generous pinch of ground cinnamon
Generous pinch of smoked paprika
½ clove garlic, diced
5ml/1 tsp fresh root ginger, chopped
2.5ml/½ tsp sesame oil
2.5ml/½ tsp Shaoxing rice wine
30g/1¼oz shiitake mushroom, cut in half
2 baby plum tomatoes, cut in quarters lengthways
40g/1½oz pork belly strips, thinly sliced
125ml/4½fl oz/½ cup stock
2.5ml/½ tsp rice wine vinegar
Pinch of sugar
Few drops light soy sauce
7g/¼oz watercress

Fennel has a long history of being really good for you, especially fennel seeds and digestion. The bonus is that combined with pork meat it tastes great! I love this simple soup, it is easy-to-make and has a wonderful homely feel.

SAUSAGE AND FENNEL SOUP

1 Add the onion, garlic, fennel seeds, diced fennel, seasoning and olive oil to a mug and microwave uncovered for 1 minute.

2 Add the sausage meat, gently fold through and microwave covered for 2 minutes.

3 Break up the cooked sausage meat in the mug and stir before adding the stock and cornflour, and then microwave uncovered for 1 minute 45 seconds.

4 Stand for a minute before garnishing with some of the fennel fronds.

CHEF'S NOTES:
You can change the flavour of this soup by trying out different types of sausage.
  Add a few chilli flakes at the end for some pockets of chilli heat!

SERVES: **1**
COOKING TIMES: **4 minutes 45 seconds, plus 1 minute standing**
EQUIPMENT: **300ml/½ pint mug**

15ml/1 tbsp finely diced onion
½ clove garlic, finely chopped
5ml/1 tsp fennel seeds
20g/¾oz fresh fennel, diced
7.5ml/1½ tsp olive oil
60g/2¼oz broken sausage meat (from approx. ½ a sausage)
185ml/6½fl oz/generous ¾ cup stock
10ml/2 tsp cornflour/ cornstarch
Chopped fresh fennel fronds, to garnish
Seasoning

I'm such a sucker for a good BBQ, so couldn't resist trying to develop a soup around some of my favourite smoky flavours. There seems like a lot of ingredients, but it's quick to make and even better to eat!

BBQ PORK AND BLACK-EYED BEAN SOUP

1 Add the spring onion, chilli, garlic, ginger, smoked paprika, oregano, ground cumin, olive oil, seasoning, black-eyed beans and pork to a mug, combine well and microwave uncovered for 2 minutes.

2 Then add the ketchup, soy sauce, honey, vinegar, stock, cornflour and coriander, and microwave uncovered for 1 minute to warm through and thicken.

3 Finish with chilli flakes, a squeeze of lime to taste, and garnish with a few extra slices of spring onion and a pinch of smoked paprika.

CHEF'S NOTES:
The soup should have a good balance of sweet and sharp; if you don't have much of a sweet tooth, save adding the honey until the end so you can add it to taste.
   This would also work exceptionally well with leftovers from an actual BBQ!

SERVES: 1
COOKING TIME: 3 minutes
EQUIPMENT: 300ml/½ pint mug

½ spring onion/scallion, sliced, plus a few extra slices to garnish
7.5ml/1½ tsp diced green jalapeño chilli
½ clove garlic, finely chopped
7.5ml/1½ tsp fresh root ginger, grated
2.5ml/½ tsp smoked paprika, plus an extra pinch to garnish
2.5ml/½ tsp dried oregano
Pinch of ground cumin

5ml/1 tsp olive oil
50g/2oz canned black-eyed beans/peas
25g/1oz minced/ground pork, broken into clumps
5ml/1 tsp ketchup
2.5ml/½ tsp dark soy sauce
2.5ml/½ tsp honey
2.5ml/½ tsp vinegar
185ml/6½fl oz/generous ¾ cup stock
5ml/1 tsp cornflour/cornstarch
5ml/1 tsp chopped fresh coriander/cilantro
Pinch of chilli flakes
Small squeeze lime juice
Seasoning

A wonderful springtime soup: lemon and lamb complement each other so well, and the addition of spinach gives vibrancy. Season well and eat slowly.

LEMON, LAMB AND SPINACH BROTH

SERVES: 1
COOKING TIME: 3 minutes
EQUIPMENT: 300ml/½ pint mug

½ spring onion/scallion, sliced
7.5ml/1½ tsp celery, diced
½ clove garlic, chopped
7.5ml/1½ tsp olive oil
2.5ml/½ tsp dried oregano

6g/¼oz spinach, chopped
30g/1¼oz minced/ground lamb
250ml/8fl oz/1 cup stock
7.5ml/1½ tsp lemon juice
7.5ml/1½ tsp cornflour/cornstarch
Chopped fresh celery leaves, to garnish
Seasoning

1 Add the spring onion, celery, garlic, olive oil and oregano to a mug and microwave uncovered for 1 minute.

2 Add the spinach, lamb (broken up to help combine) and 30ml/2 tbsp of stock and microwave uncovered for 1 minute.

3 Finally add the lemon juice, cornflour and the rest of the stock (or enough to fill the mug) and microwave uncovered for another minute.

4 Garnish with chopped fresh celery leaves and season to taste.

CHEF'S NOTES:
Taste and add more lemon juice at the end of cooking if you like.
  You could substitute celery leaves with fresh parsley.

This dark seductive soup is utterly delicious and transforms a few humble ingredients into a soup to savour. I have used some smoked bacon at the start of the recipe but you can easily omit it for a vegetarian version.

BLACK BEAN AND THYME SOUP

1 Add the bacon, spring onion, garlic, olive oil, smoked paprika, tomato purée and seasoning to a mug, mix thoroughly and microwave uncovered for 2 minutes.

2 Add the thyme, cornflour and black beans and stir thoroughly, using the back of a spoon to help mash most of the beans (this helps thicken the soup).

3 Add the stock and microwave for 1½ minutes.

4 Garnish with a sprig of thyme and an extra pinch of smoked paprika.

CHEF'S NOTES:
Add a small dollop of yogurt on top of the cooked soup to melt through, if you prefer a creamier soup.
  Replace the bacon with diced carrots for a vegetarian version.

SERVES: 1
COOKING TIME: **3½ minutes**
EQUIPMENT: **300ml/½ pint mug**

15g/½oz smoked streaky/ fatty bacon, finely diced
1 spring onion/scallion, sliced
½ clove garlic, chopped
7.5ml/1½ tsp olive oil
1.5ml/¼ tsp smoked paprika, plus extra to garnish
5ml/1 tsp tomato purée
3 fresh thyme sprigs, plus extra to garnish
5ml/1 tsp cornflour/ cornstarch
120g/4¼oz canned black beans
120ml/4fl oz/½ cup stock
Seasoning

If you are looking for a soup to warm you up in the winter months, I figure the Icelanders must know a thing or two about that!

KJOTSUPA – ICELANDIC LAMB BROTH

1 Add the onion, celery, carrot, garlic, pancetta, cabbage, olive oil, lamb, peas and thyme to a mug (break up the lamb when adding to the mug to help combine). Mix well and microwave uncovered for 3 minutes.

2 Add the oats and cornflour and mix thoroughly with the cooked ingredients before adding the stock.

3 Microwave uncovered for 1½ minutes. Season to taste.

CHEF'S NOTES:
You can also try swapping the pancetta or bacon with a smoked sausage.

SERVES: 1
COOKING TIME: 4½ minutes
EQUIPMENT: 300ml/½ pint mug

5g/¼oz onion, diced
5g/¼oz celery, diced
5g/¼oz carrot, diced
½ clove garlic, chopped
12g/½oz smoked pancetta or smoked bacon, diced
25g/1oz white cabbage, chopped
7.5ml/1½ tsp olive oil
25g/1oz minced/ground lamb
25g/1oz frozen peas
5ml/1 tsp dried thyme
15ml/1 tbsp rolled oats
7.5ml/1½ tsp cornflour/ cornstarch
100ml/3½fl oz/scant ½ cup stock
Seasoning

A lovely combination of the yin and yang, this creamy, nutty celeriac soup is peppered with cubes of salty black pudding. The secret is to mash the celeriac as much as possible.

BLACK PUDDING AND CELERIAC SOUP

SERVES: 1

COOKING TIME: 7½–8 minutes, plus 2 minutes resting

EQUIPMENT: 300ml/½ pint mug

20g/¾oz black pudding, diced
2.5ml/½ tsp olive oil
40g/1½oz potato, diced
40g/1½oz celeriac, diced
15ml/1 tbsp milk
200ml/7fl oz/scant 1 cup stock
1 bay leaf
1.5ml/¼ tsp garlic, minced
7.5ml/1½ tsp flour
30ml/2 tbsp double/heavy cream
20g/¾oz fresh breadcrumbs
Seasoning

1 First cook the black pudding by combining it with the olive oil in a mug and microwaving uncovered for 1 minute. It will clump together but don't worry – it will separate once added to the soup. Remove from the mug, reserving a few cubes for the next stage and the rest for the final stage and the garnish.

2 Add the potato, celeriac, milk, 60ml/4 tbsp stock, bay leaf, garlic and reserved few cubes of black pudding back to the mug, and place on a plate to catch the overspill. Cover and microwave for 5 minutes.

3 Remove the bay leaf and mash as much as possible with the back of a fork – the more you mash the smoother the soup will be. Add the flour and mix thoroughly before adding the remaining stock and seasoning. Microwave uncovered for 90 seconds.

4 Once cooked, stir thoroughly and add the cream, breadcrumbs and the rest of the reserved black pudding (saving a little for garnish).

5 If needed, microwave again for 30 seconds to warm through, before resting for a couple of minutes. Garnish with the last of the black pudding and season again to taste.

CHEF'S NOTES:
If you are not keen on black pudding you could try using cubes of bacon but cook them for a little longer at the start to help them crisp up.

NUTRITIONAL INFORMATION

CREAM OF TOMATO SOUP (serves 1)
Energy 336kcal/1394kJ; Protein 4.1g; Carbohydrate 12.4g, of which sugars 8.6g; Fat 30.6g, of which saturates 15.9g; Cholesterol 62mg; Calcium 63mg; Fibre 1.7g; Sodium 86mg.

CREAM OF CHICKEN SOUP (serves 1)
Energy 129kcal/538kJ; Protein 9.4g; Carbohydrate 7.5g, of which sugars 1.7g; Fat 7g, of which saturates 1.7g; Cholesterol 29mg; Calcium 23mg; Fibre 0.9g; Sodium 29mg.

MINESTRONE SOUP (serves 1) Energy 256kcal/1064kJ; Protein 14.1g; Carbohydrate 16.7g, of which sugars 5.6g; Fat 15.3g, of which saturates 5.6g; Cholesterol 27mg; Calcium 183mg; Fibre 4.8g; Sodium 389mg.

POTATO AND LEEK SOUP (serves 1) Energy 253kcal/1060kJ; Protein 4.7g; Carbohydrate 30.2g, of which sugars 3.7g; Fat 13.5g, of which saturates 8.3g; Cholesterol 67mg; Calcium 70mg; Fibre 2.8g; Sodium 118mg.

FRENCH ONION SOUP – WITH CROÛTONS (serves 1) Energy 227kcal/943kJ; Protein 5.3g; Carbohydrate 17.4g, of which sugars 4.1g; Fat 15g, of which saturates 6.8g; Cholesterol 26mg; Calcium 137mg; Fibre 1.8g; Sodium 182mg.

SMOKY PEA AND PANCETTA SOUP (serves 1) Energy 245kcal/1013kJ; Protein 15.3g; Carbohydrate 21.4g, of which sugars 4.3g; Fat 11.6g, of which saturates 4g; Cholesterol 15mg; Calcium 46mg; Fibre 11.4g; Sodium 207mg.

BROCCOLI AND BLUE CHEESE SOUP (serves 1) Energy 159kcal/666kJ; Protein 5g; Carbohydrate 16.2g, of which sugars 2g; Fat 8.7g, of which saturates 2.9g; Cholesterol 9mg; Calcium 98mg; Fibre 1.9g; Sodium 142mg.

MILAGU RASAM – INDIAN PEPPER WATER (serves 1) Energy 83kcal/343kJ; Protein 2.1g; Carbohydrate 4.7g, of which sugars 1.2g; Fat 6.5g, of which saturates 2g; Cholesterol 5mg; Calcium 35mg; Fibre 0.4g; Sodium 25mg.

CHEDDAR AND ALE SOUP (serves 1) Energy 344kcal/1433kJ; Protein 12.2g; Carbohydrate 19.7g, of which saturates 8.3g; Fat 23.2g, of which saturates 14.6g; Cholesterol 65mg; Calcium 350mg; Fibre 0.6g; Sodium 339mg.

CRUSHED PEA SOUP WITH FETA (serves 1) Energy 174kcal/722kJ; Protein 7.8g; Carbohydrate 15.8g, of which sugars 2.2g; Fat 9.3g, of which saturates 3.2g; Cholesterol 11mg; Calcium 87mg; Fibre 5g; Sodium 222mg.

SOUP-ER GREEN EGG SOUP (serves 1) Energy 202kcal/834kJ; Protein 8.9g; Carbohydrate 1.8g, of which sugars 1g; Fat 17.7g, of which saturates 3.4g; Cholesterol 212mg; Calcium 134mg; Fibre 2g; Sodium 161mg.

MEXICAN CORN AND CHIPOTLE SOUP (serves 1) Energy 245kcal/1035kJ; Protein 6g; Carbohydrate 43.1g, of which sugars 10.4g; Fat 6.6g, of which saturates 0.9g; Cholesterol 0mg; Calcium 48mg; Fibre 3.5g; Sodium 397mg.

MUSHROOM SOUP (serves 1) Energy 365kcal/1534kJ; Protein 9.7g; Carbohydrate 48.6g, of which sugars 3.1g; Fat 16g, of which saturates 9g; Cholesterol 37mg; Calcium 98mg; Fibre 3.9g; Sodium 511mg.

TRAHANA – BULGUR WHEAT AND YOGURT SOUP (serves 1) Energy 156kcal/652kJ; Protein 9.7g; Carbohydrate 6.4g, of which sugars 1.2g; Fat 10.4g, of which saturates 5.9g; Cholesterol 50mg; Calcium 74mg; Fibre 0.5g; Sodium 431mg.

FIERY SWEET POTATO AND COCONUT SOUP (serves 1) Energy 161kcal/683kJ; Protein 2.6g; Carbohydrate 27.6g, of which sugars 11.1g; Fat 6.6g, of which saturates 1.1g; Cholesterol 0mg; Calcium 104mg; Fibre 3.2g; Sodium 159mg.

RUSTIC VEGETABLE SPICED SOUP (serves 1) Energy 119kcal/499kJ; Protein 3.9g; Carbohydrate 14.2g, of which sugars 6.9g; Fat 5.7g, of which saturates 0.9g; Cholesterol 8mg; Calcium 33mg; Fibre 3.9g; Sodium 53mg.

SWEET POTATO AND ROSEMARY SOUP (serves 1) Energy 199kcal/832kJ; Protein 2g; Carbohydrate 23g, of which sugars 4.5g; Fat 11.6g, of which saturates 5.7g; Cholesterol 21mg; Calcium 36mg; Fibre 2.9g; Sodium 90mg.

MISO AND TOFU BROTH (serves 1) Energy 179kcal/747kJ; Protein 18.5g; Carbohydrate 11.5g, of which sugars 1.7g; Fat 8g, of which saturates 0.2g; Cholesterol 0mg; Calcium 149mg; Fibre 0.2g; Sodium 714mg.

BORSCHT – BEETROOT AND SOUR CREAM SOUP (serves 1) Energy 75kcal/315kJ; Protein 0.4g; Carbohydrate 11.9g, of which sugars 4.7g; Fat 3.2g, of which saturates 0.5g; Cholesterol 0mg; Calcium 28mg; Fibre 1.9g; Sodium 18mg.

PEAR, WALNUT AND BLUE CHEESE SOUP (serves 1) Energy 310kcal/1293kJ; Protein 8.6g; Carbohydrate 23.6g, of which sugars 10.4g; Fat 20.7g, of which saturates 7.8g; Cholesterol 43mg; Calcium 152mg; Fibre 4.2g; Sodium 291mg.

MOROCCAN CHICKPEA AND APRICOT SOUP (Serves 1) Energy 199kcal/838kJ; Protein 8.6g; Carbohydrate 23.9g, of which sugars 6.2g; Fat 8.5g, of which saturates 1.1g; Cholesterol 0mg; Calcium 62mg; Fibre 6.5g; Sodium 235mg.

BUTTERNUT SQUASH AND CORIANDER SOUP (serves 1) Energy 177kcal/740kJ; Protein 1.6g; Carbohydrate 18.6g, of which sugars 5.6g; Fat 11.2g, of which saturates 1.6g; Cholesterol 0mg; Calcium 78mg; Fibre 2.4g; Sodium 15mg.

ASPARAGUS AND CREAM CHEESE SOUP (serves 1) Energy 105kcal/436kJ; Protein 2.3g; Carbohydrate 8.6g, of which sugars 1.6g; Fat 7g, of which saturates 2.7g; Cholesterol 7mg; Calcium 31mg; Fibre 1.7g; Sodium 28mg.

SMOKED HADDOCK CHOWDER (serves 1) Energy 352kcal/1467kJ; Protein 21.8g; Carbohydrate 14.5g, of which sugars 2.6g; Fat 23.4g, of which saturates 13.2g; Cholesterol 111mg; Calcium 167mg; Fibre 1.1g; Sodium 969mg.

CAMBODIAN SEAFOOD SOUP (serves 1) Energy 69kcal/290kJ; Protein 12.6g; Carbohydrate 3.8g, of which sugars 3.7g; Fat 0.4g, of which saturates 0.1g; Cholesterol 137mg; Calcium 80mg; Fibre 0.4g; Sodium 491mg.

PRAWN SAGANAKI SOUP (serves 1) Energy 168kcal/699kJ; Protein 13.1g; Carbohydrate 3.4g, of which sugars 3.2g; Fat 9.6g, of which saturates 3.5g; Cholesterol 112mg; Calcium 163mg; Fibre 1.8g; Sodium 413mg.

SALMON AND TURMERIC SOUP (serves 1) Energy 236kcal/982kJ; Protein 20.4g; Carbohydrate 0.3g, of which sugars 0.3g; Fat 17g, of which saturates 2.8g; Cholesterol 50mg; Calcium 25mg; Fibre 0.2g; Sodium 46mg.

GREEK FISHERMAN'S SOUP (serves 1) Energy 192kcal/801kJ; Protein 19g; Carbohydrate 2.7g, of which sugars 2.2g; Fat 11.8g, of which saturates 1.7g; Cholesterol 46mg; Calcium 19mg; Fibre 0.7g; Sodium 80mg.

CLEANSING PRAWN NOODLE SOUP (serves 1) Energy 157kcal/661kJ; Protein 12.3g; Carbohydrate 24.9g, of which sugars 0.5g; Fat 0.5g, of which saturates 0.1g; Cholesterol 117mg; Calcium 74mg; Fibre 0.8g; Sodium 151mg.

SALMON AND DILL CREAM SOUP (serves 1) Energy 281kcal/1165kJ; Protein 17g; Carbohydrate 1.2g, of which sugars 1.1g; Fat 23.2g, of which saturates 10.5g; Cholesterol 77mg; Calcium 37mg; Fibre 0.6g; Sodium 87mg.

GREEN THAI CURRY PRAWN SOUP (serves 1) Energy 162kcal/682kJ; Protein 9.4g; Carbohydrate 19.7g, of which sugars 5.3g; Fat 5.4g, of which saturates 0.9g; Cholesterol 78mg; Calcium 63mg; Fibre 0g; Sodium 507mg.

SLOPPY JAMBALAYA (serves 1) Energy 201kcal/837kJ; Protein 10.8g; Carbohydrate 11.9g, of which sugars 3.4g; Fat 12.7g, of which saturates 1.9g; Cholesterol 78mg; Calcium 89mg; Fibre 2.2g; Sodium 102mg.

CHICKEN NOODLE SOUP (serves 1) Energy 100kcal/424kJ; Protein 7.3g; Carbohydrate 14.4g, of which sugars 0.5g; Fat 1.9g, of which saturates 0.5g; Cholesterol 20mg; Calcium 11mg; Fibre 0.9g; Sodium 54mg.

AVGOLEMONI – GREEK CHICKEN SOUP (serves 1) Energy 230kcal/966kJ; Protein 26.8g; Carbohydrate 14g, of which sugars 0.2g; Fat 7.7g, of which saturates 2.1g; Cholesterol 287mg; Calcium 42mg; Fibre 0g; Sodium 140mg.

RED CHICKEN LAKSA (serves 1) Energy 215kcal/898kJ; Protein 8.9g; Carbohydrate 19.2g, of which sugars 8.4g; Fat 11.7g, of which saturates 1.8g; Cholesterol 21mg; Calcium 38mg; Fibre 0.6g; Sodium 482mg.

CHICKEN RAMEN (serves 1) Energy 287kcal/1203kJ; Protein 19.6g; Carbohydrate 28.9g, of which sugars 12.5g; Fat 10.4g, of which saturates 2.5g; Cholesterol 259mg; Calcium 154mg; Fibre 1.9g; Sodium 693mg.

JEWISH PENICILLIN WITH TURKEY MEATBALLS (serves 1) Energy 222kcal/920kJ; Protein 10.2g; Carbohydrate 9.6g, of which sugars 2.6g; Fat 16.1g, of which saturates 2.8g; Cholesterol 28mg; Calcium 22mg; Fibre 1.4g; Sodium 97mg.

CARIBBEAN CHICKEN SOUP (serves 1) Energy 210kcal/875kJ; Protein 15g; Carbohydrate 11.1g, of which sugars 8.4g; Fat 12g, of which saturates 1.9g; Cholesterol 35mg; Calcium 116mg; Fibre 3.8g; Sodium 53mg.

CHEAT'S HARISSA BAKED BEAN CHICKEN SOUP (serves 1) Energy 185kcal/786kJ; Protein 19.7g; Carbohydrate 22.7g, of which sugars 7.5g; Fat 2.6g, of which saturates 0.5g; Cholesterol 35mg; Calcium 84mg; Fibre 6g; Sodium 722mg.

KAPUSNIAK – POLISH SAUSAGE AND CABBAGE SOUP (serves 1) Energy 150kcal/627kJ; Protein 8.8g; Carbohydrate 8g, of which sugars 2.2g; Fat 9.5g, of which saturates 3.4g; Cholesterol 33mg; Calcium 15mg; Fibre 0.8g; Sodium 547mg.

CHORIZO AND CANNELLINI BEAN SOUP (serves 1) Energy 174kcal/726kJ; Protein 9g; Carbohydrate 12.2g, of which sugars 6.2g; Fat 10.2g, of which saturates 3.3g; Cholesterol 0mg; Calcium 38mg; Fibre 4.1g; Sodium 362mg.

HOT AND SOUR SOUP (serves 1) Energy 80kcal/340kJ; Protein 6.4g; Carbohydrate 11.7g, of which sugars 7g; Fat 1.2g, of which saturates 0.4g; Cholesterol 17mg; Calcium 8mg; Fibre 0.5g; Sodium 721mg.

CALDO VERDE – PORTUGUESE CABBAGE SOUP (serves 1) Energy 84kcal/352kJ; Protein 2.5g; Carbohydrate 10.1g, of which sugars 1.1g; Fat 4g, of which saturates 1.2g; Cholesterol 10mg; Calcium 8mg; Fibre 0.8g; Sodium 63mg.

SZECHUAN HOT POT (serves 1) Energy 224kcal/927kJ; Protein 8.6g; Carbohydrate 2g, of which sugars 1.8g; Fat 20.3g, of which saturates 4.6g; Cholesterol 26mg; Calcium 40mg; Fibre 1.4g; Sodium 38mg.

SAUSAGE AND FENNEL SOUP (serves 1) Energy 269kcal/1119kJ; Protein 6.7g; Carbohydrate 18g, of which sugars 3.1g; Fat 19.4g, of which saturates 6.4g; Cholesterol 26mg; Calcium 48mg; Fibre 1.3g; Sodium 558mg.

BBQ PORK AND BLACK-EYED BEAN SOUP (serves 1) Energy 162kcal/682kJ; Protein 9.2g; Carbohydrate 19.2g, of which sugars 7.4g; Fat 5.9g, of which saturates 1.4g; Cholesterol 17mg; Calcium 53mg; Fibre 4.9g; Sodium 476mg.

LEMON, LAMB AND SPINACH BROTH (serves 1) Energy 135kcal/564kJ; Protein 6.2g; Carbohydrate 7.5g, of which sugars 0.6g; Fat 9.1g, of which saturates 2.6g; Cholesterol 23mg; Calcium 14mg; Fibre 0.4g; Sodium 26mg.

BLACK BEAN AND THYME SOUP (serves 1) Energy 231kcal/970kJ; Protein 10.9g; Carbohydrate 27.5g, of which sugars 5.4g; Fat 9.3g, of which saturates 2.1g; Cholesterol 10mg; Calcium 92mg; Fibre 10.3g; Sodium 660mg.

KJOTSUPA – ICELANDIC LAMB BROTH (serves 1) Energy 223kcal/931kJ; Protein 9.2g; Carbohydrate 21.4g, of which sugars 2.5g; Fat 11.7g, of which saturates 3g; Cholesterol 26mg; Calcium 25mg; Fibre 2.2g; Sodium 212mg.

BLACK PUDDING AND CELERIAC SOUP (serves 1) Energy 356kcal/1486kJ; Protein 7g; Carbohydrate 32.9g, of which sugars 3.2g; Fat 22.7g, of which saturates 12g; Cholesterol 64mg; Calcium 108mg; Fibre 3.4g; Sodium 373mg.

INDEX

ABOUT THE AUTHOR

Theo was born in London, has lived in America for five years and has eaten his way around the world with a backpack. His cooking first gained recognition after appearing on Masterchef 2014, where he championed Greek Cypriot-inspired 'elegant village food'. When cooking for the previous winners on Masterchef, Theo's two-course meal was well received: "every single component of both courses has been pretty much flaw-less" commented Dhruv Baker, and Natalie Coleman said "feels like there is a rave going on in my mouth... it's beautiful". Theo's formal response was; "I'm well chuffed"! Theo has a successful pop-up restaurant that sells out within minutes, serving an eight-course tasting menu, and he also runs an exclusive private dining service. He is a frequent guest chef at international restaurants and events. Theo is a regular on a BBC radio cooking show, is occasionally spotted cooking some-thing on TV – including repeat visits to ITV This Morning with *Microwave Mug Meals* (his other bestselling book!) – and can be seen demonstrating at many food festivals around the country and judging various cook-ing competitions. His website is www.TheoCooks.com.

DEDICATED TO MY WIFE ANNA AND THREE CHILDREN EVA, LEX AND LUCA

CREDITS

This edition is published by Lorenz Books, an imprint of Anness Publishing Ltd, 108 Great Russell Street, London WC1B 3NA; info@anness.com

www.lorenzbooks.com; www.annesspublishing.com; twitter: @Anness_Books

If you like the images in this book and would like to investigate using them for publishing, promotions or advertising, please visit our website www.practicalpictures.com for more information.

Publisher: Joanna Lorenz
Photography: William Shaw
Food styling: Emma Jane Frost
Prop styling: Pene Parker
Design: Adelle Mahoney
Editorial: Sarah Lumby

PUBLISHER'S NOTE
Although the advice and information in this book are believed to be accurate and true at the time of going to press, neither the authors nor the publisher can accept any legal responsibility or liability for any errors or omissions that may have been made nor for any inaccuracies nor for any loss, harm or injury that comes about from following instructions or advice in this book. Always refer to your microwave's handbook for usage advice.

COOK'S NOTES

For all recipes, quantities are given in both metric and imperial measures and, where appropriate, in standard cups and spoons. Follow one set of measures, but not a mixture, because they are not interchangeable. Standard spoon and cup measures are level. 1 tsp = 5ml, 1 tbsp = 15ml, 1 cup = 250ml/8fl oz.
Australian standard tablespoons are 20ml. Australian readers should use 3 tsp in place of 1 tbsp for measuring small quantities. American pints are 16fl oz/2 cups. American readers should use 20fl oz/2.5 cups in place of 1 pint when measuring liquids.
The nutritional analysis given for each recipe is calculated per portion (i.e. serving or item), unless otherwise stated. If the recipe gives a range, such as Serves 4–6, then the nutritional analysis will be for the smaller portion size, i.e. 6 servings. The analysis does not include optional ingredients, such as salt added to taste. Medium (US large) eggs are used unless otherwise stated.